D0773679

A Gaia **Busy Person's** Guide

Crystals

Simple routines for home, work, & travel

Christina Rodenbeck

Gaia Books

A Gaia Original

Books from Gaia celebrate the vision of Gaia, the self-sustaining living earth, and seek to help its readers live in greater personal and planetary harmony.

Editor	Christina Rodenbeck
Project Editor	Camilla Davis
Design	Peggy Sadler
Art Direction	Patrick Nugent
Editorial Direction	Jo Godfrey Wood
Production	Simone Nauerth
Photography	Ruth Jenkinson

® This is a Registered Trade Mark of Gaia Books
an imprint of Octopus Publishing Group
2–4 Heron Quays, London, E14 4JP

First published in Great Britain in 2006 by Gaia Books

Copyright © Gaia Books 2006

Distributed in the United States and Canada by
Sterling Publishing Co., Inc.
387 Park Avenue South, New York, NY 10016–8810

All rights reserved. No part of this work may be reproduced or utilized in any form or by any means, electronic or mechanical, including photocopying, recording or by any information storage and retrieval systems, without the prior written permission of the publisher

ISBN-13 9 781856 752565
ISBN 1 85675 256 9

A catalogue record of this book is available from the British Library

Printed and bound in China

10 9 8 7 6 5 4 3 2 1

CAUTION

This book is not intended to replace medical care under the direct supervision of a qualified doctor. Before embarking on any changes in your health regime, consult your doctor. While all the exercises detailed in this book are extremely safe if done correctly, you must seek professional advice if you are in any doubt about any medical condition.

Contents

Introduction

You have opened this book, so you are entering a glorious Aladdin's Cave, where colours whisper secrets and crystals have amazing healing powers, where sparkle and glitter hide stores of wisdom.

Although crystal lore is old, perhaps as old as humankind itself, it has taken on many new layers in the modern era – which can be hard for both novice and expert to sort through.

It is an area that abounds with mumbo jumbo and hocus pocus. Together we can explore some of the myriad passageways, cul-de-sacs and odd ante-chambers of the crystal world, finding out what really works and what might just be a load of old rocks.

This user-friendly guide is your companion in the world of crystals, providing sensible advice and practical know-how. It is designed for the solo voyager, keen to explore on his or her own, although there may be occasions when you need to ask a partner to participate in some of the exercises. By the time you have finished reading it, you should have an excellent grounding in the principles of crystal work and feel confident enough to strike out on your own.

Working with crystals is particularly suited to the 21st century, since it can easily be slotted into a busy life. It helps if you can put aside a few minutes every day to at least touch your crystals, and perhaps spend a few moments focusing on them. But for the most part you will find your crystals ideal companions, silently working away for you as you get on with other things – nice to look at and responsive to your touch when the mood takes you.

HOW TO USE THIS BOOK

As with any guidebook, you are free to choose just how to use it to meet your needs. You can read it from cover to cover, starting at the beginning and going on to the end. This will give you the best foundation for further practice and study, as along the way you will learn all the basics of working with crystals from testing and caring for your crystals to particular healing techniques and layout to using crystals to stabilize the atmosphere of your home.

BELOW *(from the left) aquamarine, turquoise, sodalite (centre top), lapis lazuli (centre bottom), celestite*

However, this book is also meant to be dipped into as a ready reference. It's a handy problem solver, meant to be used as an everyday manual for crystal work. Instead of having to plough through hundreds of words on each crystal, you can turn straight to a particular problem and implement the suggested cure. If you have a particular issue to be fixed, such as depression, a shortage of money or a lacklustre love life, you will find a crystal remedy within these pages.

If you do need a quick, pithy understanding of the properties of any of the most popular crystals available, then you should turn to the Crystal Directory on pages 138–41. When you go out crystal shopping, you may want to take this book with you.

This book will work in tandem with the crystals that you find, own, and personalize. For example, your rose quartz may well turn out to be excellent for encouraging loving vibrations as suggested on page 98, but it may also be good for soothing headaches. Naturally, your personality and circumstances will affect the outcome of the work, but the more able you are to switch off and allow the crystals to work for you, the more effective will be your results.

YOUR CONTRIBUTION

Working with crystals is a fascinating experience. You need to allow your imagination to wander and your intuition to flow – but at the same time, you should maintain a certain amount of detached scientific rigour. Remember, imagination does not equal emotional investment.

View all of your work with crystals as part of an ongoing personal experiment. There are no hard and fast rules about which crystals work in which context. Crystals are highly individuated healing tools – sensitive to you, the emotional or physical situation, and the environment. You need to pay close attention when you are using them, keeping all of your intuitive faculties highly tuned, but also retaining enough scientific cool to step back and ask yourself if you have really achieved a result. Keeping a notebook of your crystal work is an excellent way of reminding yourself of what works and what does not. Eventually you will create a resource that will be useful for years to come – especially since it will be uniquely tailored to your own personal crystal collection.

So, as you set out on this crystal journey, travel light. Throw out your burden of preconceptions, wishes, and fears, and allow the crystals themselves to light the way for you.

Christine

CHAPTER ONE

Introducing crystals

For as long as human beings have walked this planet, we have been fascinated by certain mysterious and beautiful stones. Created in the dark heart of the earth, crystals are a miracle of colour and light, and so they have been treasured by people of all cultures.

Most crystals were made by geological action over hundreds of thousands of years. Before being mined, some may have lain hidden in the earth for millions of years – even since the very formation of the planet. So when you hold a crystal in the palm of your hand, you are touching something beyond history, an object that transcends time itself.

Prehistoric people were certainly fascinated by the precious and semi-precious stones, or crystals, of the earth. Archaeology shows that certain crystals, such as jade, were valued above others. But their worth was more than intrinsic. In ancient times – and in most of the world today still – the gems set into jewellery serve more than a decorative purpose; they are also amuletic – warding off evil or attracting good.

Today, there is a revival in interest and belief in the healing power of crystals. There is very little scientific evidence to back up these ideas, but the actual experience of many healers and their clients, as well as many lay users of crystals, tells a different story. It is up to you to explore the world of crystals for yourself and see how they can transform your life.

What is a crystal?

When chemical compounds or elements change from a liquid or vapour into a solid they usually take the form of crystals. In the process of solidification, the crystal develops geometrically, so the smallest particle has the same inner structure as the largest – salt and sugar are familiar examples of crystalline chemicals. In this book we will be focusing on crystals that are formed in this way and are used for healing, magic, and personal development. They are those crystals that you generally find in shops labelled as crystals.

The atomic structure of crystals is what determines their shape. They can be made up of a single element – for example diamonds are pure carbon – or a combination. But the pattern in which the atoms join together, know as the lattice, is always consistent within a crystal type – this is how they are classified. For example, like diamonds, coal is pure carbon, but its lattice is completely different.

In the shop, crystals may look fairly similar in terms of shape. This is because many crystals are sold after they have been tumbled smooth, so you can't see their natural form with the naked eye.

Although crystals of the same family, say quartz, will always have the same inner structure, they may well come in a wide variety of colours – and even shapes. Some very valuable stones, such as rubies, are close first cousins to commoners such as hematite.

RIGHT *amethyst geode*

How do crystals work?

Crystals are some of the simplest and most stable structures in the known universe – this may well be what gives them their power. They are made of repeated patterns of atoms or groups of atoms – molecules –connected together in a strong matrix.

Certain unique properties of crystals may explain why they work. First of all, all material is made up of a variety of different types of molecules that come together to create a single entity. For example, you are made up of an incredible variety of molecules that work together to create cells that create your unique self. Even, say, a pot of soil will contain many different types of minerals and vegetables that are jumbled together.

Secondly, many crystals – in particular quartz – contain a type of energy called piezoelectricity, which is due to floating positively charged sub-atomic particles trapped in the inner structure of the lattice. Piezoelectricity is released when the crystal is mechanically squeezed or subjected to an electric field – the crystal itself remains unaltered. Piezo-electricity is a result of the crystal's very simple basic structure, which may also be the key to how these crystals help us.

Sometimes only a very little bit of mechanical intervention can release this energy. Try rubbing a piece of amber and observe the static electricity you have made. This property is used in engineering, for example, quartz watches and radio transmitters. The piezoelectric charge generated using quartz is so precise that it is used to keep Greenwich Mean Time.

But most crystals, by contrast, are simply one atom or molecule repeated ad infinitum. This means that on an electromagnetic level, each crystal gives off a single, consistent type of energy. Compare this with yourself – sometimes you're fast, sometimes you're slow, sometimes you're asleep, sometimes you're awake. You mind, body, and spirit work in rhythms and cycles – sometimes not all that consistently either.

So a crystal may work as a kind of sub-atomic metronome, giving your body a steady, dependable rhythm to lock into.

CRYSTAL ENERGY
The energy or piezoelectric charge released from the crystal quartz is so precise that it is used in watches to keep time.

Crystal geometry

Crystals are among the most symmetrical objects in creation, and tend to be symmetrical along all axes. This means there are actually only seven basic shapes that a crystal can take. These shapes are how geologists classify crystals, and they also give healers some ideas about how crystals can be used. Of course, there are always some exceptions to any rule and these are the amorphous crystals.

BELOW *(from the top left clockwise) moonstone, obsidian, sodalite, aquamarine, bloodstone, rhodalite, (centre) peridot*

CRYSTAL MATRICES

Shape	Inner structure	Potential uses	Sample crystals
Cubic	Square	Practical, down-to-earth	Rock salt, sodalite
Tetragonal	Rectangular	Balancing opposites	Rutile, zircon
Orthorhombic	Rhombic	Purification, cleansing	Peridot, topaz
Trigonal	Triangular	Energy boosters	Amethyst, bloodstone
Monoclinic	Parallelogram	Clearing obstructions	Jade, moonstone
Triclinic	Trapezoid	Accessing higher states of consciousness	Rhodonite, turquoise
Hexagonal	Hexagon	Growth	Quartz, aquamarine
Amorphous		Creativity	Amber, opal, obsidian

Crystals and colour

Crystals come in a rainbow spectrum of colours from the blackest onyx to the clear limpidity of a real diamond. In fact, we often refer to crystals in descriptions of colour such as carnelian, turquoise, ruby, sapphire blue, green, emerald, and amber.

Colours are a result of the combination of minerals within the crystal structure. Some crystals, such as malachite, are coloured because of the chemical composition of the crystal lattice itself. In the case of malachite, it is the presence of copper that causes the deep sea-green. Others are tinted because of slight impurities in the crystal lattice. Aventurine is a type of quartz that gets its pale green shade from hematite or mica impurities. Commercially processed crystals are also often subjected to high heat to create colour.

Objects refract or absorb different parts of the colour spectrum, from red to indigo, according to their composition. So, for example, when we see a citrine as pale yellow, this is because all the other colours of the rainbow have been absorbed by the crystal. The one colour that is refracted is yellow. Clear crystals refract the entire spectrum, while deep-black ones absorb it.

CLEAR QUARTZ
Cut clear quartz crystal may refract a rainbow of light.

History and crystals

We live in an age of specialization. It's only in modern times that we have come to delineate a big difference between doctors, healers, magicians, scientists, and astrologers. Previously, all these roles might well have been taken by one member of the tribe – the sage, wiseman or woman, shaman, or seer. This person would likely have had some knowledge of the use of crystals in all his or her roles.

EGYPTIAN AMULET
A pendant in the shape of a boat carrying a scarab, the symbol of the gods resurrection, flanked by two royal serpents. This is from the tomb of the Egyptian pharaoh, Tutankhamun.

Crystals have been used in medicine, as amulets and as spiritual and psychic tools, since time immemorial. Jade has been found in prehistoric tombs, as well as black obsidian shaped into mirrors very similar to those used by modern scryers. Amber was also highly prized and routes were established across Europe to trade in it.

The royal blue stone lapis lazuli was clearly highly valued across Central Asia and the Indian sub-continent well before written history began. It has been found in tombs dating back 7,000 years in the Indus Valley. By 4500 BC, mining lapis lazuli had become an industrial process at Tell-i-Bakun in Persia.

It was not until the rise of civilizations in the Ancient Near East that we have written records of how humans used crystals. The Egyptians were fond of all kinds of crystals, especially blue ones such as turquoise mined in the Sinai Peninsula, and lapis lazuli, which was associated with the goddess Isis. Precious and semi-precious stones, or crystals, were used in the making of amulets to attract luck, ward off the evil eye, or bring fertility. Bloodstone was said to help to open locked doors.

Egyptian doctors at the time were also priests, and one of their jobs was to create amulets and spells for health. Surviving medical papyri explain how to use certain stones. For example, topaz, dedicated to the sun god Ra, was prescribed to relieve rheumatism. It seems that poultices and medicines were seen mainly as painkillers, while the cure itself was thought to be effected by magic.

Meanwhile, the Chinese were already developing a passion for jade that was to last for millennia. Jade artefacts from the Songze culture (4500–3000 BC) can be seen today in the History Museum at Beijing. Jade was said to confer health, wealth, and longevity. Even the search for jade was surrounded by taboos – only women were allowed to do it.

HISTORICAL PERSPECTIVE

The Indian tradition of gemology, which is still followed today (see Indian Astrology pp. 130–1), is extremely ancient. And like much Hindu lore, it has been written down and studied for many centuries – probably since about the first century AD. The art of studying and prescribing crystals was known as *ratnapariska*, as it is described in the Hame Sutra (c.700 BC). The most powerful amulet prescribed in ancient Hindu texts is the *navaratna* or nine-gem jewel. It is made up of a ruby, an emerald, a pearl, a coral, a jacinth, a tiger's eye, a topaz, a sapphire, and a diamond – each representing one of the seven planets and the north and south nodes of the moon.

In the Western tradition, the first written record we have of the medicinal use of crystals is in the treatise "On Stones" by the Greek philosopher Theophrastus (372–286 BC), who was Aristotle's successor as head of the Peripatetic School in Athens. Theophrastus, a prolific classifier of the natural world, was the first to attempt to organize crystals into groups and describe them. He divided them into "male" and "female" crystals, which was later to cause some confusion, and he also assigned both medicinal and magical properties to some of them.

BIBLE STORY

Crystals are often mentioned in the Bible, but usually only as a means of describing colour or great wealth. However, God gave precise instructions about the construction of the mysterious Breastplate of Judgement, which was to be worn by the high priest of Israel. No one knows what the precise significance of each stone was meant to be.

"And thou shalt make the breastplate of judgment with cunning work; after the work of the ephod thou shalt make it: of gold, of blue, and of purple, and of scarlet, and of fine twined linen, shalt thou make it.

Foursquare it shall be being doubled; a span shall be the length thereof, and a span shall be the breadth thereof.

And thou shalt set in it settings of stones, even four rows of stones: the first row shall be a sardius, a topaz, and a carbuncle: this shall be the first row.

And the second row shall be an emerald, a sapphire, and a diamond.

And the third row a ligure, an agate, and an amethyst.

And the fourth row a beryl, and an onyx, and a jasper: they shall be set in gold in their inclosings.

And the stones shall be with the names of the children of Israel, twelve, according to their names, like the engravings of a signet; every one with his name shall they be according to the twelve tribes."
Exodus 28: 15–21

RIGHT *A Jewish High Priest in his ceremonial clothes.*

A ROMAN CURE FOR DELIRIUM

"Amber, however, is not without its utility in a medicinal point of view; though it is not for this reason that the women are so pleased with it. It is beneficial for infants also, attached to the body in the form of an amulet; and, according to Callistratus, it is good for any age, as a preventive of delirium and as a cure for strangury, either taken in drink or attached as an amulet to the body."
Pliny the Elder (AD 23–79), Natural History

LEFT *An amber carving of a bear dated as the first century* AD.

The knowledge of the Greeks was added to and embellished over the next 1,500 years or so in a series of books and treatises on crystals, or as they were more commonly called, precious and semi-precious stones, called lapidaries. These contain a mixture of geological, magical, and medical lore.

Possibly the most influential work was Pliny the Elder's *Natural History*. Written in the first century AD, it was to influence scholars and medical practitioners well into the next millennia. Pliny was a voracious collector of data, who liked to include a touch of gossip, opinion, innuendo, and hearsay in most of his discussions of the natural world. This makes his

PLANETARY AMULETS

The planets were believed to rule certain stones, plants, and animals. These were combined to create magical talismans to fortify the wearer with the characteristics assigned to that planet.

- *Sun – amber, chrysolite, topaz*
- *Moon – beryl, diamond, mother of pearl, opal, quartz*
- *Mercury – agate, carnelian, chalcedony, sardonyx*

- *Venus – emerald, jade*
- *Mars – bloodstone, hematite, jasper, ruby*
- *Jupiter – amethyst, aquamarine, blue diamond, sapphire, turquoise*
- *Saturn – jet, obsidian, onyx*

ABOVE *(from top left, clockwise) smoky quartz, red jasper, onyx, amber, jade, carnelian (centre) amethyst*

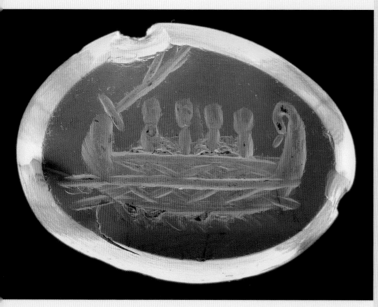

MAGICAL ENGRAVINGS
The Book of Wings, *written in the 13th century by someone using the name Raziel, explains how each gem should be engraved to make its magic more powerful. Here is an extract: "The figure of a falcon, if on a topaz, helps to acquire the good will of kings, princes, and magnates …The well-formed image of a lion, if engraved on a garnet will protect and preserve honour and health, cures the wearer of all diseases, brings him honors and guards him from all perils in travelling."*

LEFT *A ring, from the third century* AD, *with an intaglio design depicting a Roman warship.*

Natural History entertaining, but somewhat dubious as a sourcebook.

In the 11th century the *Book of Stones*, written by Mabodus, Bishop of Rennes, was something of an international bestseller, since it was translated from Latin into eight other European languages.

But it is Hildegard von Bingen (1098–1171) who probably most influenced modern crystal healers. Her book, *Physica*, details the natural history and curative properties of stones, herbs, and animals. In it, she also recommends recipes and explains certain folk cures.

ELIXIRS AND POTIONS
Medieval lapidaries recommend either elixirs of
particular crystals or the ground powder of certain
others for medicinal purposes. One Pope was said to
have swallowed a king's ransom in precious stones at
a sitting.

Crystals were also assigned special meanings that
would have been quite widely known at the time.
For example, Pope Innocent III sent King John of
England four rings: the sapphire to represent hope;
the emerald, faith; the garnet, charity; and the topaz,
good works – none of which did him much good in
the end.

The magical properties of precious stones were
also thought to be enhanced by engraving. Precious
stones – usually engraved with emblems, animals,
or astrological symbols – were widely prescribed as
amulets. The tradition was thought to date back to
Ancient Egypt, and some of the symbols used – such
as the scarab on an emerald – were certainly of Near
Eastern origin.

A PASSION FOR CRYSTAL
*"I find it stated by medical men that the very
best cautery for the human body is a ball of
crystal acted upon by the rays of the sun.
This substance, too, has been made the
object of a mania; for, not many years ago,
a mistress of a family, who was by no means
very rich, gave one hundred and fifty
thousand sesterces for a single basin made of
crystal. Nero, on receiving tidings that all
was lost, in the excess of his fury, dashed two
cups of crystal to pieces; this being his last
act of vengeance upon his fellow-creatures,
preventing any one from ever drinking again
from these vessels." Pliny the Elder (AD 23–79),*
Natural History

Crystals today

Since the rise of interest in alternative medicine, new spirituality, and personal development in the 20th century, greater curiosity about the potential uses of crystals has developed. Some of this attention is based on the rediscovery of old lapidaries and magical treatises; much of this new regard is based on the re-evaluation of non-Western traditions, such as those of the Native American shaman and the Aboriginal "clever fellows", and particularly Ayurvedic medicine as practised in India today.

It is important to remember, though, as you begin your exploration of the world of crystals, that a lot of

NATIVE AMERICAN HEALERS

Although the tribes of North America have diverse belief systems, in general they hold that a Universal Spirit imbues everything – animal, mineral, and vegetable. So for the medicine man or woman, the powers of certain minerals is vital in healing rituals.

The approach to healing is holistic – often based on the idea of good and bad energy or good and bad spirit. This fits in well with current thinking about crystal healing.

Some medicine men and women have a special crystal, known as a totem stone, that they use in healing. It may be placed on the body of the patient to draw out bad energy, or simply carried and its vibrations used to help the healer.

In some tribes, members have totem stones, which they carry for protection and to reinforce a connection to the Universal Spirit.

They are also used in the creation of the Medicine Wheel, which represents the passing year. One stone is assigned to each lunar month, so dates are approximate. The stones listed below are probably modern rather than traditional. Your birth month will tell you which is your totem stone.

December 22 to January 19 – quartz
January 20 to February 18 – silver
February 19 to March 20 – turquoise
March 21 to April 19 – fire opal
April 20 to May 20 – chrysocolla
May 21 to June 20 – moss agate
June 21 to July 22 – rose quartz, carnelian
July 23 to August 22 – garnet
August 23 to September 22 – amethyst
September 23 to October 23 – jasper
October 24 to November 21 – malachite
November 22 to December 21 – obsidian

the claims made for crystals are as yet unproved – and some are positively far-fetched.

Roughly, the uses of crystals can be broken down into three categories: physical healing or protection; emotional or mental support and healing; and spiritual and psychic growth and protection.

CLEVER FELLOWS

Much of the oral tradition of the Aboriginal Australians is unavailable to outsiders. It is considered secret knowledge, passed on from father to son or mother to daughter, and kept within the tribe.

What data we do have is either considered unimportant by the Aboriginals themselves or is thanks to the work of anthropologists, who have been allowed to observe some of the shamanic rituals of Australia's "clever fellows". During these rituals, some of the men appeared to be pulling quartz crystals in great quantities out of their mouths. Whether or not this was sleight of hand, we don't know. What is certain is that the crystal is an important part of religious initiation.

When a child is born a sacred stone, called a churinga, *is inscribed and placed in a cave, where it will protect and help the child for the rest of his life. Examples of* churingas *survive from the Stone Age.*

One example of an Aboriginal healing crystal is mookaite, a kind of quartz oxide, that is good for regeneration, wound healing, and strength.

ABOVE *Churinga*

PHYSICAL HEALING

Alternative medicine is often at its best when used to heal chronic conditions, such as arthritis – or certain conditions that conventional doctors simply find hard to diagnose. It also works well as an adjunct to orthodox treatments. For example, if you break a leg, you would probably like to have it set by a doctor, and you might like to take some painkillers prescribed by her, but to enhance the healing process, you could wear malachite or meditate with calcite regularly.

Professional healers who use crystals usually have their own tried and tested battery of crystals – personalized by years of use. Reflexologists or masseuses may swear by a few well-used crystals – an amethyst or clear quartz, say – for helping to relax the muscles. Alternative midwives occasionally use healing stones in the labour room. These crystals are said to focus healing energy on the patient.

For your personal use, crystals should only ever be used as an extra, never as a substitute for qualified professional attention. Furthermore, you should always view your own efforts as an experiment: if you think a crystal is making you feel peculiar, then stop using it. Having said that, many practitioners report that the first three days of wearing or laying on of crystals (see above right) may make you feel worse before you start feeling any benefit.

LAYING ON
Crystal healers usually put crystals on and around the patient's body. The vibrations of the crystals are used to rebalance and harmonize the patient's own natural ability to heal.

EMOTIONAL AND MENTAL HEALING AND SUPPORT

Crystals work well with the subtle energies of our moods and emotions. They can provide a steadying guidance when we are fighting our way through the emotional jungle, and comfort if we fall into a depressive bog. If you are prone to mood swings, one of the grounding crystals (see p. 48), such as black tourmaline or tiger's eye, carried in your hip pocket may be all that you need to keep going.

Because of their consistent electric energy, crystals can facilitate clear thinking – very useful when writing books or studying for exams. Discordant atmospheres can be calmed using crystals; places where energy seems to have slowed down to a sluggish dribble can be jazzed up.

CONTINUOUS CALM
Wearing a crystal bracelet is a simple and effective means of carrying positive energy with you.

SPIRITUAL AND PSYCHIC AWARENESS

The purity and simplicity of crystals can provide a straight and steady connection to the world of the spirit – no matter what your belief system. They can also enhance our awareness of the infinite mystery that is life in a positive way – and help us to connect appropriately to that mystery.

The best way to start exploring a crystal's numinous connection is to spend time meditating with it. The vibration between you and the crystal is unique but repeatable, so that if you find that you respond very well to a particular crystal the first time, it should become easier and more effective the more you use it.

In general, violet, white, or transparent crystals are connected with the spiritual plane. Try using angelite, amethyst, or clear quartz to begin with.

AMULETS

It's true to say that in most of the world today jewellery still has a sacred or amuletic purpose that is deemed more important than its decorative use. The most widely used amuletic crystal is turquoise, which is treasured by Native Americans, Tibetans, and other tribes of Central Asia. Because of its colour, turquoise is associated with the sky, rain, and water. It also has a tendency to change colour with age, which makes it almost seem like a living creature.

The red carnelian also has a long tradition of use as an amulet, particularly in Central Asia, where it is the most popular magical crystal – it is associated with blood and the worship of fire, passion, and the universal life energy that permeates all things.

Jade is still popular in China today, where its magical ability to attract prosperity and health is valued as much as its beauty. The simple jade pi – a disc with a hole through the centre – is worn as a protective amulet all over the Far East.

MEDITATING WITH CRYSTALS

Crystals are a great tool for keeping the mind focused during meditation. You can either touch or simply look at a crystal when you are meditating. What is important is to allow yourself to enter the right state of mind first. A good crystal to start with is clear quartz, but as you become more experienced, you will want to choose crystals to meditate with that have the energy that suits your needs or mood of the moment.

■ Find a quiet place where you will not be disturbed. Make sure your clothing is loose and comfortable, and that you will not be too hot or too cold if you sit still for half an hour or so. You may want to wrap yourself in a thin blanket, as many people find that they cool down when they are meditating.

■ Choose one crystal. If you intend to look at it, place it close so that you can easily see it without having to move. If you are holding it, keep it in your left hand.

■ Once you have picked your spot, get into a comfortable position. If you can sit cross-legged without pain for a long period, then try that. Most people, though, will find that sitting in an upright chair is perfectly good. Lying down to meditate is also good, but you may need to fight the tendency to drift off to sleep.

■ If you are sitting, make sure that your spine is straight, but not like a ramrod. You should feel as if your head is floating on top of your spine; everything should feel loose and flexible. This is important for your breathing: the key to meditation.

■ Take a few deep breaths in through your nose. Let your breath fill your lungs. Imagine that you are expanding your lungs to the back as well as the front. Let the air out slowly.

■ Now consciously relax your body, starting with your toes and working up. You can do this quite quickly, imagining that you are letting go of tension with each exhalation.

■ Now that you are completely relaxed, notice your breath gently sliding in and out of your nostrils. It should be quite delicate.

■ Focus on your crystal. Allow its colour to enfold you. Feel its energy around you. Lose yourself in the crystal. If you are just gazing, allow your eyes to go out of focus. Every time your thoughts begin to drift, return to the crystal.

■ If you are holding your crystal, allow its energy and colour to spread up your arm, into your body and fill the air around you. Again, every time your mind begins to drift, return to the crystal energy.

■ When you have finished, drink a large glass of water and give yourself time to come back to the world.

RIGHT *The crystal used in this picture is labradorite.*

CHAPTER TWO

Getting started

The world of crystals is an Aladdin's cave of glowing light and colour – but it can be confusing in there. At first you may feel you want one of every crystal, but tune in to your intuition and you will find that you may only need a few crystal.

Choosing crystals is enormous fun. After all, most of them are gorgeous to look at and deliciously tactile. It's easy to get carried away, stroking and caressing glistening piles of crystals in a shop or at a fair, and this is how most of us acquire our crystal toolkit. If you're a keen amateur geologist and you live near some good sites, you may want to consider collecting crystals outdoors.

Because of the allure of crystals, some people end up with enormous hunks of glistening rock that dominate their homes. Too much crystal scattered around your house can create a very chaotic vibration – especially if you live in a small place. So it's important when you're starting to take things slowly and see how you and your crystals interact on a vibrational level. Quite often it's a case of less is more.

Once you've acquired a few crystals, you need to take care of them correctly, keeping them clean and in good running order. All crystals will need a regular checkup, just like any other tool you keep in your box.

Beginning with optimism

Why not start your collection with a single crystal that brings you joy? Make this a "wake up and smell the coffee" crystal; a crystal that you want to look at first thing in the morning; a crystal that makes you leap out of bed feeling energetic, lively, and focused.

The first crystal you choose is crucial. It will set the tone for the whole enterprise – creating a special energy in your home that will work with each new one you acquire.

WAKE UP AND SMELL THE COFFEE CRYSTALS

Crystal	Effects
Beryl (yellow, golden)	Dynamism, clear-sightedness, optimism
Citrine	Self-confidence, individuality, mental stimulation
Emerald	Harmony, truthfulness, trust
Fire opal	Success, sexual energy, inner fire, high spirits
Garnet (red, pink, or orange)	Courage, joy, grabbing the future
Ruby	Fire, pure energy, joy
Green tourmaline (verdelite)	A sense of wonder, joy

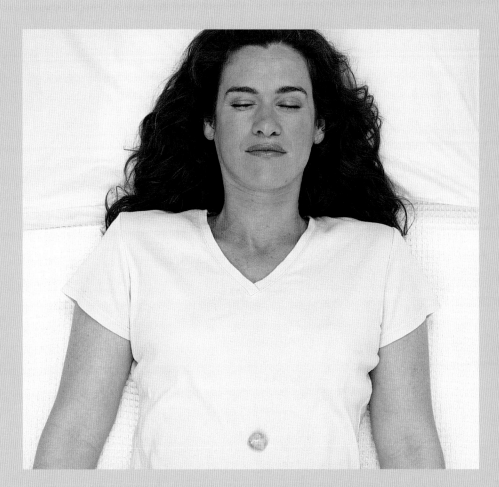

MORNING MEDITATION

Keep your crystal beside your bed. As soon as you wake up, take it and put it on your solar plexus (see p. 68–9). Close your eyes and focus your mind on the healing energy emanating from the stone through your body. Imagine the colour of your crystal as a warm glow that spreads through your body from the top of your head to the tips of your toes. Now imagine it filling the air around you – float there for a while. When you are ready, open your eyes and start your day.

ABOVE *The crystal used in this picture is citrine.*

Choosing your crystals

Putting together a crystal toolkit should be fun – and not too expensive. First of all, you should take a look at any crystals that you may already own. That means looking at all your jewellery. Some practitioners say that a crystal with a hole doesn't work, but this does not seem to hold true. You may be surprised to find out just how many crystals you have floating around your home. Try to identify your crystals. If you cannot, take them to a jeweller who will do it for you.

Now check to see if any of the crystals you already own are useful to you. You may be surprised to find that you are already wearing one – a diamond perhaps – that does serve a need. The crystals you already own are powerful because they are imbued with your energy.

Next you will need to acquire some clear quartz. This is the most versatile and useful of all rocks, so you should get quartz in various shapes. Don't bother pursuing rarer examples, but a set of, say, four single-terminated clear quartz crystals (points) will come in handy time and time again. In fact, you may find that this is all you need as the "points" will effectively channel energy towards the tips. You will be able to use them for all kinds of mental, emotional, and even physical healing; for cleansing other crystals and even for Feng Shui.

SINGLE-TERMINATED CRYSTALS
Also known as points, these crystals are used to direct energy. In order to draw negative energy away from the body, aim the points outward. To draw positive energy in, point them toward the subject.

DOUBLE-TERMINATED CRYSTALS
These crystals have two definite points so the energy is channelled, radiated or absorbed in two directions simultaneously.

USING INTUITION

When you step into a crystal emporium, you may well find yourself paralyzed by too much choice, although you should already have some ideas about which types of crystal you need.

- Don't think about anything as you drift around the shop or fair. Make sure you are breathing slowly but steadily through your nose – the idea is to put yourself in a semi-meditative state. Try to relax your mind.
- Usually the crystals are displayed in baskets or *en masse*, with the more expensive crystals shown individually. Focus on the smaller crystals first – there's no point spending a fortune on crystals right away. You should be aiming to build your collection gradually.
- Allow your left hand to pass over the receptacle containing the kind of crystal you want. See if you feel pulled to take one. If not move on to the next heap of crystals and come back later.
- If you start to think about the crystals, gently push the thought away. Allow your hands and fingers to do all the choosing for you.
- Some people talk about the crystal calling to them. It's almost as if they can hear the tiny vibrations emitted by the crystal.

DOS AND DON'TS WHEN CRYSTAL SHOPPING

Do
- *Take your time*
- *Use your intuition*
- *Enjoy yourself*
- *Touch the crystals*
- *Get sidetracked*
- *Be prepared to give away crystals that don't work for you*

Don't
- *Be seduced by big, glittery crystals*
- *Feel that the more you pay, the better the crystals*
- *Go mad with your cheque-book and buy the shop*
- *Forget that you can always come back another time*

FORMS AND VARIATIONS
Crystals come in all shapes and sizes – from great rough rocks to delicately worked jewellery.

ROUGH OR RAW CRYSTALS
Crystals in their natural state often have very powerful vibrations that can change the atmosphere of a whole room. The energy tends to be gentle, natural, and diffused.

LEFT *onyx*

POINTS OR WANDS
Also known as single- and double-terminated crystals. Check to see if the point is naturally occurring or whether it has been worked – some practitioners believe that natural points are more effective. This type of crystal is an energy transmitter and excellent for healing.

LEFT *single-terminated clear quartz*

CLUSTERS AND GEODES

These also produce high energy. Large clusters or geodes (hollows filled with crystal) are powerful energy generators and can sometimes have an overwhelming effect in a small space. Tiny crystal clusters have good healing energy when laid on the body.

LEFT *amethyst*

TUMBLED STONES

These have been polished in a machine. The effect is that the energy radiates more evenly, so they are excellent for laying on the body or carrying in your pocket.

LEFT *(left to right) clear, rose, smoky quartz*

SLICES

These often reveal the inner beauty of a crystal structure. In traditional crystal healing, if the shape thus revealed corresponds with a particular part of the body, it is specially powerful. Slices are good for laying on or for wearing in jewellery.

LEFT *agate, dyed mauve*

Set of starter crystals

Start with a few crystals and gradually expand your collection – you shouldn't feel in any hurry. The selection here is a good start, because these crystals will address the most common problems you come across. They are easy to get hold of and, as a rule, are reasonably priced and versatile. But do not feel bound to start with them. If you are unaccountably drawn to some other crystals, choose those. However, the idea is to achieve a fairly balanced selection of crystals rather than having a whole bunch that only offer a similar set of solutions.

BASIC CRYSTAL SET
Agate (blue, grey, green, and brown)
- *Good luck and protection*
- *Growth, stability, and maturity*

Blue lace agate
- *Feminine energy*
- *Harmony*

Moss agate
- *Green fingers*
- *Making new friends*

Amethyst (violet)
- *Harmony, enlightenment, and connection to spirit*
- *Wisdom and tolerance*
- *Good for meditation*

Carnelian – also known as sard (red, orange, yellow, and brown)
- *Courage and action*
- *Ability to finish projects*
- *Physical energy*

Citrine (yellow)
- *Confidence; anti-depressant*
- *Mental clarity, dynamism, and initiative*
- *Good digestion*

Clear quartz
- *Focusing energy of all kinds*
- *As a stand-in for any other crystal*
- *Simple tumbled clear quartz is fine, but try to get hold of some quartz points as they will prove invaluable*

Lapis lazuli (dark blue)
- Wisdom, kindness, and love
- Protection from negative energy
- Peace and harmony

Malachite (dark green)
- Prosperity, money luck, and sensual appreciation
- Healing past hurt
- For stimulating healing dreams and revealing subconscious yearning

Obsidian (black)
- Insight
- Grounding and protection from negative influences
- Dissolving pain

Peridot (green)
- Mental, emotional, and physical detox
- Healing
- Used in the Middle Ages to ward off evil spirits

Red jasper
- Courage
- Grounding
- Physical strength and sexual energy
- Honesty
- Speed energy up
- Yellow jasper has a calmer energy and green jasper has a more balanced energy

Rose quartz (pink)
- Love
- Self-healing and love

Smoky quartz (pale grey to dark brown)
- Grounding and protection against bad luck
- Dissolving pain
- A couple of single- or double-terminated crystals would be useful as well as a simple tumbled stone

Sodalite
- Wisdom and insight
- Listening and speaking skills
- Organisation
- Counters harmful radiation

Tiger's eye
- Protection and grounding
- Trust and common sense
- Slows energy down
- Good for starting new ventures with both feet on the ground

Turquoise
- Protection – particularly from ill-wishers and on long journeys
- Connection to spirit
- Mentally and spiritually uplifting
- One of the most widely used crystals for amulets

Grounding

Grounding is a term that is regularly use these days. Essentially, it means keeping a grip on reality by maintaining your connection to the earth. If you ever engage in any spiritual work or healing, it's important to make sure you are grounded when you finish – try stamping your feet or drinking a glass of water. When you are working with crystals, always use a grounding crystal as part of your set.

Many of us – especially sensitive types – find it quite difficult to stay grounded in the everyday. We have a tendency to daydream or let our mind drift off when we should be concentrating on matters at hand. This is exacerbated by the unnatural pace of modern life. Simply carrying one of the grounding crystals in your pocket can work wonders.

WHEN GROUNDING CAN HELP
You may need to work on grounding if:
- Your relationships don't last.
- Your career is just a job.
- You can't make your mind up and have trouble focusing on the project in hand.
- You jump from fad to fad.
- You daydream a lot.
- You often feel sort of 'floaty'.
- You feel you are a drifter.
- You attract emotional leeches.

GOOD GROUNDING CRYSTALS
- *Boji stones*
- *Black tourmaline*
- *Hematite*
- *Jet*
- *Obsidian*
- *Red jasper*
- *Smoky quartz*
- *Tiger's eye*

GROUNDING EXERCISE

Allow yourself some time with this exercise initially. But as you get the hang of it, it should only take you a minute or two to feel grounded. You may literally feel a pleasant kind of downward-pulling energy.

- *Sit somewhere comfortable where you will not be disturbed.*
- *Hold a grounding crystal in each hand, and rest them gently on your thighs.*
- *Close your eyes and focus on your breathing. Watch the air flowing gently in and out of your nostrils.*
- *With each exhalation, imagine that thoughts and ideas are emptying from your mind. With each inhalation, imagine a clear light sweeping through your body and bringing in clean, new energy.*
- *When you are feeling refreshed, feel the energy of the crystals in your two hands. Feel it flowing up your arms and filling your torso. Feel it flowing down your body and through your spine into the floor. Feel it flowing through each leg and down through the soles of your feet. Imagine this energy rooting into the earth, connecting you right down into the soil like a tree. If you are good at visualizing, imagine yourself growing these roots.*
- *You are now fully grounded. When you are ready, open your eyes and carry on with your crystal work.*

RIGHT *The crystals used in this picture are hematite.*

Testing your crystals

You can test your reaction to specific crystals using a technique called kinesiology. You may have come across kinesiology in relation to food allergies. It requires a partner to work with, but it's by far the clearest way of checking your reaction to the many different crystals available.

This system is sometimes called muscle-testing, because it relies on checking the strength or weakness of your right arm muscles. A crystal that agrees with you will strengthen your muscles or have no effect, while one that saps your energy will weaken them.

THE TEST
(01) Standing up straight, but comfortably, stretch your right arm from the shoulder horizontally. Hold it so that it is flexible, but not floppy.

01/02

03/04

(02) Using her right palm, your partner should push gently down on your arm and see how much resistance she meets. This will give her an idea of what your natural resistance is to being pushed.

(03) Hold the crystal to be tested in your left hand at waist height. Give it a little time to warm up.

(04) When you are ready, hold your right arm out again, and let your partner push gently down in the same way as before. If she meets more resistance than before, take this as a "yes" the crystal agrees with you. Your arm may even bounce up a little when she lets go. If your arm seems to have become more relaxed, that's a "no".

Caring for your crystals

The crystals you have are a precious gift and it's up to you to look after them and keep them in top condition. This means keeping them in a sensible place, adjusting their programming when necessary, and cleansing them.

CLEANSING A CRYSTAL

When crystal healers talk of cleansing a stone, they mean more than getting rid of any dirt. What you are doing is clearing the energy of the crystal and helping its unique vibration to resonate effectively.

RUNNING WATER

Holding a crystal under a tap is often enough to refresh the crystal. Put it under cold running water – either keep the crystal in your hand or put it in a glass receptacle and let the water wash over it. Halite and selenite are actually water-soluble, so this solution won't do. Lapis lazuli, malachite, and turquoise should never be soaked.

ABOVE *quartz amethyst*

ROCK OR SEA SALT

Salt can be quite harmful to some crystals – for example opal is ruined by contact with salt; however, it is a highly effective cleansing agent. To use the salt energy without affecting the crystal, put the crystal in a glass dish and then embed the dish in the salt. Leave it for a day or more.

ABOVE *hematite*

When you first acquire a crystal you should cleanse it thoroughly. This is especially true if you bought it from a shop or if it was previously used by someone else. A good wash in soapy water should be your first step, if only to get rid of any accumulated grease and grime. The exception is if you found the crystals yourself in its true environment – on a river bed or in the earth, for example. If the latter is the case, you may want to retain the vibes of its place of origin. If you are able to return to the crystal's place of origin once in a while, you may want to take it along with you for a little refreshment.

SEA OR SALT WATER

Clean sea water is a wonderful cleanser – especially if you have a crystal that you feel is very damaged. If you can't get hold of any sea water, try mineral water mixed with sea salt. Be generous with the salt, and leave the crystal in the salt water overnight. Some practitioners swear by putting the container in the light of the full Moon.

ABOVE *rhodonite*

SUNLIGHT

Leaving the crystal in the full light of the sun will also energize the stone. It is an especially useful method for those crystals that already have a sunny energy, such as citrine, ruby, or sunstone. Amethyst, rose quartz, and turquoise sometimes fade in sunlight, so this method is not suitable for them.

ABOVE *sunstone*

SMOKE

Native Americans traditionally cleansed their crystals
with white sage or sagebrush
smoke. Sage for "smudging"
is fairly easy to get hold of in
shops. Simply light the sage
and either allow the crystal
to sit in the smoke or pass it
through the smoke.

LEFT *smoking sagebush and
sodalite*

BIG ROCK

Leaving a crystal in the nest
of a crystal cluster can help
readjust its vibrations, but
be sure the cluster is itself
OK. Amethyst and quartz
clusters are especially
favoured for this method of
cleansing. A set of single-
terminated clear quartz
crystals pointing inward in
a circle around the crystal to
be cleansed also works.

ABOVE *amethyst cluster with
raspberry garnet*

SOUND

Clear sound vibrations are an excellent way of tuning a crystal – a singing bowl will clear a group of crystals in minutes. Simply put the crystals in the bowl then tap it and allow the note to resonate through the stones. You can do the same with a tuning fork by holding it next to a single crystal. Theoretically, anyone with a good singing voice should be able to purify a crystal by maintaining a single pure note. This could also be a good way of truly personalizing your collection.

STORING CRYSTALS

While it is nice to keep some crystals on display in your home, be careful of jumbling up a lot of different crystal vibrations in your living space. The result can be anything but harmonious – they will also need more regular cleaning. It's best to keep most crystals stored in a safe place, out of the light. Also, laying a carnelian in with the other stones will help keep them cleansed and tuned.

Many crystals are quite fragile, especially those that have not been tumbled smooth – a lined jewellery box is an ideal storage place. Special crystals should be kept wrapped in their own cloth and only brought out for special purposes, and any crystals with points or fissures should be kept separately.

BAG OF CRYSTALS

A soft leather pouch is a traditional place for keeping tumbled crystals, especially if you do any travelling with your crystals, as the leather helps contain the crystal vibrations. But you may want to fashion your own pouch out of silk or some other soft, natural fibre. Be careful not to put any delicate crystals in with their more robust brothers and sisters, because they may get damaged.

ABOVE *(from top left clockwise) chyrsoprase, yellow jasper, celestite, carnelian*

TUNING AND PROGRAMMING

Each of your crystals is sending out a subtle electro-magnetic vibration; each is doing its own thing. Because the lattice of each crystal is such a simple structure, the vibrations of a crystal are especially pure and consistent – which may be what gives them their special and unique healing properties. You should remember this when you start to programme your crystals.

First of all, be sure that the purpose you have chosen for the particular crystal is an appropriate one: a fire opal is unlikely to be much good at calming a situation down for instance; and all the will-power in the world won't force an agate to become a warrior.

Next, think about the exact purpose you have in mind for this crystal – the clearer your intention, the more effective the programming. Try to think up a precise phrase that sums up what you want to do with this crystal. For example, "I want to enhance family harmony", or "I want this crystal to promote open communications".

Then, take the crystal in your left hand and feel it warm against your skin. See if you can sense the single-note vibration coming from the stone. Think about how it feels. Check to see if your intended purpose for the crystal fits the crystal.

Next, say your phrase out loud, as the voice is always more effective than the mind alone. But if you are shy about it, simply repeat the phrase in your mind.

You may have to repeat this process several times, but you will find that the more you use the phrase for its special purpose, the more effective it becomes.

CHAPTER THREE

Healing

No one is quite sure how crystals work with the
human body – whether the effect is psychological or
physical or perhaps some even more mysterious
connection. What is sure is that for some people,
crystals laid on the body have a beneficial effect.

In the West, the art of crystal healing is in its infancy. Influenced chiefly by Native American, Indian, and pre-Renaissance European traditions, Western healers started experimenting early last century with the laying on of crystals (see p. 32), and for most of those years crystal healing was seen as very much a fringe activity.

By the 1990s, some more orthodox practitioners were using crystals regularly, and finding them subtly effective. Crystals used in conjunction with other alternative treatments – acupressure, hypnotherapy, massage, and reflexology – seemed to work especially well.

However, as with all holistic medicine – therapy that treats the whole person – it is almost impossible to run proper trials as you would for a drug, since each case is unique as each person is unique.

This means that although particular crystals are recommended for certain conditions, and particular layouts also, you must treat each case individually.

Crystal healing is intuitive. There are no set rules, so you should view all your efforts as experiments. Take notes to remind yourself of what works and what does not. It's a good idea to keep a special notebook for your records, and in time you will build up a useful resource.

Furthermore, take any very rigid advice on which crystals you should use with a pinch of salt – it may just not work for you.

Healing with crystals

Laying crystals on or around the body for healing is a wholly intuitive process, but there are certain principles to keep in mind when you use this technique. The point of healing with crystals is to either draw in or expel positive or negative energy. The specific type of energy required to do this is provided by the crystal, and the placement of your choosen crystal determines where the energy will be focused.

It is really a matter of common sense deciding whether your chief need is to expel negative energy or to absorb positive energy – usually, healing requires a combination of the two. For example, if you are dealing with depression, you will want to drain the negative feelings of worthlessness, but you need to replace those with joy or wholeheartedness.

Single- or double-terminated crystals are specially effective for directing energy to or from the body. If you want to use only one healing crystal, a single- or double-terminated clear quartz may well be sufficient.

WORKING WITH PARTNERS

You may find that working together with someone else achieves better results for you. One of you acts as the healer and the other as the subject. Not everyone can heal, and it is sometimes surprising to find out who is a natural.

There are certain measures you must take to deal with the powerful energies that you encounter during a healing session. Both the healer and the subject should make sure that they are well grounded (see

WANDS
Many crystals come in the shape of a wand. These may be naturally occurring or man-made. Wands are said to be particularly effective for focusing and directing energy like a laser beam. The most versatile wand is quartz crystal, but you should experiment with others when you are out crystal shopping. You may find that an earthy energy like obsidian or smoky quartz, suits you better; or maybe a gentle harmonizing energy, such as amethyst or rose quartz. Some prac-titioners favour tourmaline wands, which come in a wide variety of colours, because they pinpoint energy so accurately.

Grounding pp. 48–9), and are feeling centred and calm before starting a session. The healer should simply see themselves as a channel for energy – the mind and emotions should feel quite neutral. If you are too emotionally involved in the session, things could go wrong.

Most healers feel light pouring in through the top of their head and out through their hands when they are working. To achieve this, meditate beforehand, focusing on opening your crown chakra (see pp. 68–9) and allowing the energy to flow in – the energy may only start to flow when you begin the session. For an experienced person this may only take a moment.

It is most important that you do not retain or absorb any negative energy from the subject. After you have finished a session, make sure you do a grounding visualization that expels bad energy. Try visualizing a red cord from your feet that connects you to the centre of the earth. Send all the bad energy down the cord and imagine it as black waste. When the cord returns to a ruby red colour, you have discharged all the energy.

FLUORITE STROKES
If you feel there are a few areas of weakness in your aura's outer membrane, try taking a fluorite crystal or wand and stroke the areas of your aura that need healing (see pp. 72–3). Do this standing up, then focus and meditate on your aura.

Liquid crystals

Gem or crystal elixirs are easy to make, and you may find that they are an effective way of absorbing a particular crystal's vibrations. You can either ingest them, drop a very minute amount on the affected spot, or add them to your bath water.

Some practitioners swear by them, but there's not much evidence that their effect is anything other than psychological. Some Ayurvedic astrologers regularly prescribe elixirs as a kind of gemstone remedy. Try them out and see if you can feel any effect.

MAKING AN ELIXIR

Put the crystal in a glass of mineral or spring water, and leave it to stand in the sun for all the hours of daylight of one day. Remove the crystal and pour the elixir in to a dark glass bottle with an airtight stopper.

Use seven drops of the elixir three times a day on the affected spot or add a dash to your bath water. Alternatively, dilute the seven drops of elixir in a glass of water; be sure that your crystal is non-toxic.

BATHING IN CRYSTALS

A delicious way of absorbing crystal vibrations is by taking a bath with crystals. Put your crystal under the tap as you are running your bath, get in, close your eyes, and relax. Try to meditate a little, clearing your mind and allowing the crystal's energy to flow around and through you.

CRYSTALS THAT SHOULD NOT BE USED IN ELIXIRS
Some crystals contain toxic material, so you should check to make sure your crystal is safe to use. The following do not work well as elixirs:
- *Halite*
- *Selenite*
- *Lapis lazuli*
- *Malachite*
- *Turquoise*

BLUE LACE AGATE ELIXIR
Traditionally used for its healing, cleansing, and neutralizing properties, blue lace agate (pictured right) is also used as a suitable eye elixir for eye strain and aching eyes.

Working with colour

Much theory about how crystals affect us is simply based on their hue, therefore an understanding of colour will help you make sense of the whole field. So if you want to go on to experiment with crystals, it's important to have an understanding of the effects of colour on you and anyone you may work with.

Understanding the influence of the different colours will enhance your healing powers enormously – and help you to make accurate decisions about which crystals to use.

Remember that colour therapists find that although there may be certain general rules with colours, each person has an individual reaction. For instance, if you have always had a favourite colour, you may well find that the qualities associated with it are ones you especially admire – or perhaps lack.

Colours do have overlapping meanings. For example, blue promotes self-expression and therefore communication, whereas yellow helps more general interaction with other people. You must use your common sense to decide whether to concentrate on one or several different colours at any one time.

As well as taking colour into account when you are choosing which crystals to use for a healing, try lying on a cloth of a particular colour when you are practising a therapy. As you develop your crystal collection, try to have at least two crystals in each colour range, as you may find certain crystals work more effectively for specific problems.

BASIC COLOUR CRYSTAL SET

Colour	Sample crystals
Red	Carnelian, red jasper
Pink	Rose quartz, pink tourmaline, rhodochrosite
Orange	Amber, citrine
Yellow	Agate, yellow jasper, amber, citrine
Green	Aventurine, malachite, moss agate
Blue	Blue lace agate, turquoise, lapis lazuli, sodalite
Purple	Amethyst, fluorite, alexandrite
Black/Brown	Obsidian, onyx, smoky quartz, tiger's eye
White/Colourless	Quartz, opal, moonstone

THE EFFECTS OF COLOUR

White
Purifying, cleansing, enlightening, clarifying, and neutralizing.

Red
Physically stimulating, sexually arousing; encourages action, energy, lust, passion, and strength.

Pink
Sympathy, love, and harmony.

Orange
Creatively stimulating; encourages joie de vivre and a sense of well-being; good for the sex organs, fertility, and confidence.

Yellow
Mentally stimulating; enhances sense of personal power, validation and self-worth; counters depression; helps digestion and communication.

Green
Healing, love, and harmony; emotional and physical detox; helps with emotional connection to others; de-stressing; stimulates the liver.

Blue
Relaxation, tranquillity, and calm; helps with the balance of chemicals in the body; stimulates the kidneys and bladder.

Purple/Violet
Peace; clairvoyance, intuition, and spiritual matters; brain activity; cleanses lungs and skin.

Black/Brown
Absorbing negative energy; connection to earth energy; elimination of pain.

Understanding Chakras

The basis of much crystal healing is an understanding of the chakra system that is used in traditional Indian Ayurvedic medicine. The chakras, "wheels" in Sanskrit, are spinning balls of energy within your body.

Like Chinese medicine, Ayurvedic medicine is based on the idea that we should be pulling in fresh, clean energy and expelling negative, used-up energy. The chakras are like a series of cogs running up your spine, continuously renewing your energy.

In a well-balanced and healthy person, the chakras are spinning rapidly and smoothly, and if you visualize them their colours are fairly clear – they should be about the same size as a grapefruit. When someone is mentally, emotionally, or physically unwell, the chakras start to spin either too fast or too slow; they discolour or fragment; enlarge or contract.

Most of us have some chakra misalignment most of the time – after all nobody's perfect. The aim of healing using the chakras is to get the system working more smoothly and evenly.

There are seven main chakras, although many people claim there is an eighth above the crown chakra. There are also smaller chakras in other parts of the body. For healing, the most important of these minor chakras are those located in the hands, since these are connected to the heart chakra – you should be very aware of them if you are healing someone else. There are also two small ones in the feet connected to the root chakra. Being aware of these chakras will help you to stay grounded during your healing sessions.

CHAKRA CLEANSER
A simple but effective crystal layout for the chakras is to put one single-terminated crystal above your head pointing downward and one at your feet pointing upward; visualize energy running smoothly between the crystals up and down through your chakras.

CHAKRA TESTING

If you are working with another person, you can try muscle-testing using the appropriate crystal (see pp. 50–1) to check the health of each chakra. There are two other simple techniques you can also try:

- *Touch. If you are working with someone else, see if you can feel her chakras. It is easier if the subject stands, but this also works lying down. Take a few breaths and feel yourself grounding. Focus on your own*

hands and feel them warm up. Start to move them very slowly up and down about 8 cm (3 in) away from the other person's body. At each chakra you should be able to feel warmth or coolness, strength or weakness (see above).
- *Visualization. Sit as if you are about to meditate and close your eyes. When you feel relaxed, visualize each chakra in turn, and check it with your mind's eye. Check for colour, size, speed of spin, and whether its edges are fuzzy or smooth.*

THE SEVEN CHAKRAS

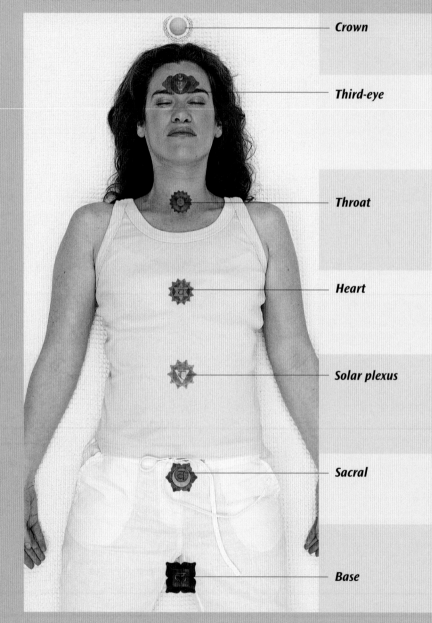

Crown

Third-eye

Throat

Heart

Solar plexus

Sacral

Base

Colour: Violet
Benefits: Spiritual enlightenment, connection
to the source

Associated sense: Transcendence
Crystals: Mainly clear, violet
Examples: Diamond, clear quartz, amethyst

Colour: Indigo
Benefits: Second-sight, clear thinking,
knowledge, intuition, wisdom
Associated sense: Sixth-sense

Crystals: mainly purple, dark blue
Examples: Lapis lazuli, sodalite, amethyst,
fluorite

Colour: Blue
Benefits: Communication, openness to
receiving as well as giving information, self-
expression

Associated sense: Hearing
Crystals: Mainly blue
Examples: Aquamarine, turquoise, celestite,
blue lace agate, sapphire

Colour: Green
Benefits: Love, relationships, sharing
Associated sense: touch

Crystals: Mainly green, pink
Examples: Jade, aventurine, watermelon
tourmaline, rose quartz

Colour: Yellow
Benefits: Sense of self, boundaries,
assertiveness, will, taking action
Associated sense: Sight

Crystals: Mainly yellow, gold
Examples: Yellow amber, lemon citrine,
sunstone, malachite

Colour: Orange
Benefits: Creativity, fertility, making manifest
Associated sense: Taste

Crystals: Mainly orange, gold, amber
Examples: Orange amber, golden topaz,
moonstone, carnelian, orange citrine

Colour: Red
Benefits: Connection to the earth, survival
instinct
Associated sense: Smell

Crystals: Mainly red, mauve, brown and
black
Examples: Agate, bloodstone, tiger's eye,
hematite, onyx, obsidian, carnelian,
sardonyx

REBALANCING THE CHAKRAS

Understanding the correspondences between crystals and chakras will help you in choosing crystals to carry, wear, or keep in the house. If you feel a weakness in a certain area of your life, check which chakra that might be affecting and wear an appropriate crystal near it. For example, if you have trouble making yourself heard at work, try wearing a blue crystal, such as a blue lace agate, around your neck.

RIGHT *(from top to bottom) amethyst, lapis lazuli, blue lace agate, aventurine, yellow amber, carnelian, bloodstone*

Rebalancing the chakras takes time and energy, so set aside an hour or two in which to do this exercise, when you will not be disturbed. Whether you are doing it for yourself or someone else, make sure you are well-grounded before you start. If you are doing it for someone else, you should wear a grounding crystal such as hematite or smoky quartz (see pp. 48–9).

CHAKRA REBALANCING

- Make sure your crystals are cleansed, charged and programmed for chakra healing (see pp. 52–7). When programming them, simply fill your mind with love and healing and allow that to flow freely into the crystals.
- Lie comfortably on the floor or on a bed. This healing works best if the crystals have skin contact, so you will want to wear loose clothing, placing the crystals underneath.
- Starting with the base, place a single appropriate crystal on each chakra (see opposite). You may want to hold a heart chakra crystal loosely in each hand.
- Close your eyes and start breathing gently through your nose. Focus on the breath moving in and out of your body.

- Now, as you breathe in, breathe from the very bottom of your body. Visualize yourself breathing in positive energy from the base crystal.
- As you breathe out, feel that energy travelling up through your body and out.
- The cycle of breath is setting your base chakra turning. See if you can visualize this both the chakra and the motion.
- Do the same with each chakra. You may find that your chakras spin in opposite directions like gears. Feel the energy from each individual chakra first – and then feel them all working together.
- You should feel highly energized after this healing, but don't go flying around. Stay indoors and do something grounding such as eating a meal or taking a bath.

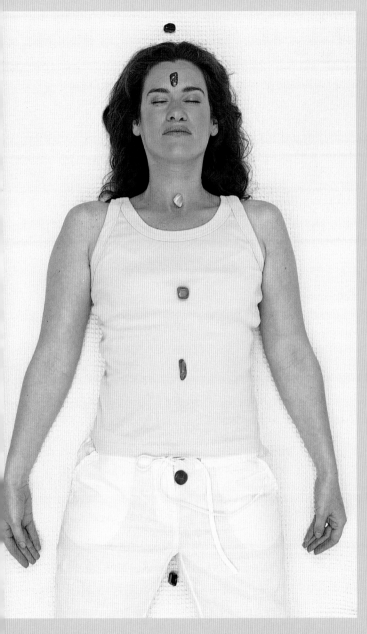

OTHER WAYS OF EXPLORING CHAKRAS

Instead of doing a full chakra layout, you may want to concentrate on one or two chakras that are giving you trouble.

Following are several options to try. With these techniques, you may want to also place a crown chakra crystal above your head and a grounding crystal below your feet.

- *Use three single-terminated clear quartz crystals, in a circle centred on one particular chakra.*
- *Choose four to six crystals that relate to a single chakra and lay them out in a circle. They may all be different or all the same.*
- *Simply put one crystal on one chakra and focus all your attention on that.*

Or try wearing chakra crystals:

- *Wear one appropriate crystal over the chakra for a week.*
- *Wear a single-terminated crystal aiming downward over the chakra for a day.*
- *Carry the appropriate crystal in a pocket and touch it whenever you feel overwhelmed.*

Healing your aura

If you find chakras a hard concept to swallow, then you may need to take a deep breath before you start even contemplating cleansing your aura. The fact is most people, no matter how hard they try, are never going to see an aura – so it's a little hard to believe they exist.

However, surprisingly enough, most people can feel an aura quite easily, given the right circumstances. Once you have felt an aura or two, it is much easier to start visualizing them in your mind's eye, and whole new worlds will open up to you.

The aura is an energy field around a person's body. There are basically four layers to it, but they are rarely clearly demarcated as shown in our diagram (see opposite) – the layers tend to blend into each other. True clairvoyants can often see all the layers of an aura and the chakras, too. The "physical aura" is simply the warm energy field around a person – and anyone should be able to feel that without trying. Think about when you shake hands or stand close to someone.

VISUALIZING YOUR AURA

- *Relax, clear your mind, and breathe calmly. Close your eyes.*
- *Now imagine your aura. You may find that it is full of many colours and not layered at all. You may see swirls or clouds like coloured gas.*
- *Allow the colours to come and go.*
- *See if you can see the outer membrane of your aura. It may be like a big, rainbow-hued soap bubble.*

CRYSTALS FOR AURAS

- *Amethyst – draws in spiritual energy, heals holes, cleanses*
- *Apache tear – protects*
- *Bloodstone – cleans rapidly*
- *Fluorite – strengthens aura's membrane, creating a shield*
- *Green Tourmaline – heals damaged aura*
- *Jet – protects*
- *Magnetite – strengthens*
- *Quartz – cleanses, protects, energizes*
- *Smoky quartz – cleanses, grounds negative energies*

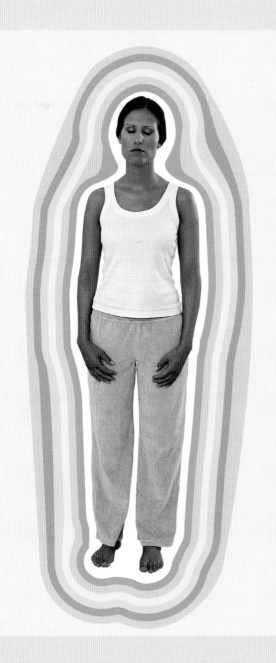

AURA LAYERS
The layers of a person's aura usually blend into each other. The layer of warm energy right next to the body is often visible as white light, but other parts of the aura are more often invisible to the naked eye.

FEELING AN AURA

The outer layers are harder to feel separately, but on the very outside of the aura, there is a thin skin, like a membrane. This skin should be smooth and without holes, since it is what protects the person from too much negative energy. Auras typically develop tears and holes when a person is feeling disturbed, and crystals are used to repair these holes as you would patch a damaged tent.

You need to do this exercise with another person, when you are both feeling relaxed and comfortable. Both of you should follow the directions for relaxation before you start.

- Sitting or standing, relax completely. With your eyes closed, work through your body from top to bottom, making sure each muscle is released.
- Check your breathing. Make sure you are breathing – quite gently – to the very bottom of your lungs. Try doing this by focusing on breathing right down into your lower back.
- Take about ten cycles of inhaling and exhaling. Don't gasp for air. This should be gentle and the flow or air smooth.
- As you breathe, you should find that your mind is clearing of all thoughts. Try to simply concentrate on your breath in order to give your brain a rest.
- When you are ready, open your eyes and stand up. Your partner should also be standing and feeling relaxed. Your partner may want to keep his or her eyes closed, just to test the results of this experiment.
- Slowly start to walk towards your partner with your hands outstretched, but relaxed.
- About 1 m (3 ft) from your partner, you will feel slight resistance. Stop there and feel up and down. You will feel a wall of energy almost like a membrane around your partner – and he or she should feel you touch it too.
- Try this experiment a few times and you will find that it comes quite easily. You will also find that you can visualize the colours of a person's aura more easily now when you shut your eyes.

HEALING A DAMAGED AURA

Even if you are not convinced about auras, this layout is very good for anyone feeling generally run-down, out of sorts, or depressed.

- Cleanse and programme nine single-terminated clear quartz crystals and one smoky quartz to heal your aura (see pp. 52–7).

- Either on your bed or on the floor, lay out the crystals, with the points facing in, so that you will be able to carefully lie down surrounded by them. Ideally they should be about 75 cm (29 in) away from your body. (Crystals shown closer here due to space limitations.) Put one clear quartz crystal directly above your head and the smoky quartz at your feet. Place the others in evenly spaced pairs around your body.

- Now, lie down surrounded by the crystals. Close your eyes, clear your mind of any conscious thoughts, relax your body completely, and gently breathe gently in and out through your nose. Feel the positive energy of the quartz crystals clearing your auric field. Imagine all the negative energy that is there being sucked up by the smoky quartz and sent down into the earth.

- Synchronize your inhalations with the positive energy that you are drawing in from the crystals, and your exhalations with the negative energy being expelled.
- If you have any gaps or tears in your aura, focus on them. Imagine the light from the crystals closing the holes.
- Allow yourself as long as you want for this healing, but afterwards make sure you do some grounding work (see pp. 48–9).

Layouts & crystals for specific problems

Crystal healing works best when it is focused on alleviating emotional distress, chronic blockage or excess of energy, or as illness that might have a psychological basis. Crystals are not a cure for acute conditions, although they can help to alleviate pain.

All the layouts included here should be left for at least 15 minutes. They are designed so that you can use them on yourself without having to involve anyone else. Feel free to adapt them in any way that you feel is suitable. When placing crystals around the body, put them about one handspan away from it.

Crystals can become more powerful if they are used repeatedly for the same purpose.

HEALING A BROKEN HEART

The gentle vibrations of crystals act as a balm for the broken hearted. If you have suffered a severe loss through death or a messy break-up, all the energies in your body will be out of alignment. Grief prostrates us mentally, physically, and emotionally, disconnecting us temporarily from everything we knew before. Try this layout and adapt it to suit you. It is worth repeating regularly.

- *Place a circle of single-terminated clear quartz out around the body. These are to draw away the grief.*
- *Place one sugilite over the third eye. Sugilite is one of the great heart-healing crystal that reconnects us with the loving spirit. If you cannot find sugilite substitute amethyst, which is also a beautiful crystal.*
- *Over the heart chakra place one rose quartz or watermelon tourmaline to heal the break.*
- *Place one malachite on the solar plexus to help heal your broken heart and also protect it. When we are grief stricken, we are also vulnerable.*
- *At your feet place a grounding crystal (see p. 48) to help draw away negativity and reconnect you to the earth.*

DETOX

Green stones are particularly associated with detox. Often they work by helping to stimulate liver and kidneys, which eliminate waste. You may want to try this layout in combination with a detox programme.

- *Place one or more peridot crystals where the legs join the torso – this is one of the best detoxing stones. Try moving it around the body to find the spot where you can feel its effects most.*
- *Place one single-terminated clear quartz on the solar plexus pointing downwards.*

Alternative detox crystals:

- *Azurite*
- *Chrysoprase*
- *Emerald*
- *Green jasper*
- *Green opal*
- *Green tourmaline*
- *Magnesite*
- *Malachite*
- *Turquoise*

BEATING STRESS

It's true that many of us respond well to stressful situations, often needing a certain amount of tension to perform at peak level. But problems start if we never learn how to wind down. We need to learn how to manage our stress levels and how to keep them at a comfortable level. This layout is designed to help you wind down, so it is good to come back to it regularly.

Another simple solution is to place a double-terminated clear quartz crystal on your chest pointing to your head and your feet. This will help disperse the blocked energy that's causing your stress.

- *Place one apophyllite on the solar plexus. This is a real healer's crystal that absorbs stress and rebalances energy.*
- *On the base chakra place one obsidian, black tourmaline, or another black crystal. This will help to absorb negative energy.*
- *Position one lapis lazuli on the forehead to create calm. Alternatively, fluorite placed here will help the body to reorganize its energy flow.*
- *If you feel the stress has built up in a particular area of the body, place two single-terminated clear quartz crystals near to the affected area, and pointing outward from either side of your body .*

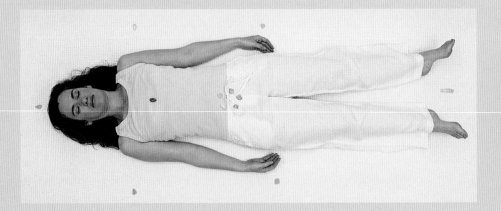

FERTILITY, CHILDBIRTH, AND PREGNANCY

The connection between procreation and crystals is as old as human history. In many parts of the world, from the Imperial Court at Pekin (Beijing) to the Amazon basin, green crystals were worn by women to promote fertility. In particular jade was considered to have magical properties.

Jade, moonstone, thulite, and rose quartz are just some of the crystals said to boost fertility. If you are trying to conceive, put one of these under your mattress. You could also try gridding the bed with green crystals (see pp. 88–9).

Moonstone is also closely associated with the female cycle. It is said to help with menstrual cramps and pregnancy. Wearing a carnelian is said to prevent miscarriage and agate is said to help protect both mother and baby during pregnancy.

There are also certain crystals said to facilitate giving birth, including amazonite, jade, malachite, moon-stone, moss agate, opal, and peridot. Slip some of these into your hospital bag or have them handy if you plan on a home birth. Try rubbing your belly with one or get your birth partner to stroke your back with one.

This layout aims to stimulate the reproductive organs and the emotions of harmony and love that create the best conditions for making babies.

- Place five rose quartzes around the body including one straight above the head. This is to bring in loving vibrations.
- Place one clear quartz at the feet. If using a single-terminated, point it upward. A double-terminated is even better – this will draw in earth energy.
- On the sacral chakra place a ring of moonstones.
- On your heart chakra place one green or pink crystal, such as amazonite, jade, rose quartz, or rhodonite.

DEPRESSION

There are many causes of depression, and it is good to know the root cause of your condition. Is it physical? For example, seasonal affective disorder. Is it emotional? Your heart has been broken. Is it spiritual? You feel lost and aimless. When you know the cause you can focus on the relevant chakra. However, here is a general healing layout that should help uplift you and move you forward.

- *Surround the body with a combination of clear single-terminated quartz facing out, and single-terminated citrine facing in. If you only have one citrine, put it directly above the head. This will bring in warm, life-giving energy and draw out any negative energy.*
- *Place one peridot on the third eye. This is a very power healing stone – placed here it will have the effect of detoxifying negative thinking patterns. If you do not have a peridot, try a sugilite. This will create a feeling of calm.*
- *Place one moss agate at the base of the throat and over the heart. This will help to heal old wounds and to release self-pity.*

Extra help

- *Amber, tiger's eye, and citrine, or some other combination of orange and yellow crystals, in a line from the sacral chakra to the solar plexus will help to reinvigorate you with a love of life.*
- *Jasper or rhodochrosite on the base chakra will re-energize you. One of the troubles with depression is falling into a cycle of lassitude, so getting the physical body moving is an important part of recovery.*

Treating common physical ailments

Crystals should never be a substitute for a doctor's advice, but they can aid cures that you are already using. They are especially effective for chronic conditions such as fatigue.

COMMON AILMENTS

All-round healing
In general green crystals often help the healing process. Specifically, peridot, garnet, rhodonite, and sapphire are good for all round healing and boosting the immune system.

Arthritis
Fluorite placed on the spot or a grossular garnet in a bath.

Asthma
Carry apophyllite with you. During an attack hold it to your chest. WARNING: do not substitute this crystal for any more conventional cures that you are using. This is additional.

Backache
Ask someone to gently stroke the affected area with smoky obsidian or smoky quartz.

Chronic pain
In general, black crystals dissolve pain.

Chronic fatigue
Ametrine, apatite, citrine, green tourmaline, and rutilated quartz are all said to alleviate chronic fatigue. Wear them continuously, and so that they touch the skin – maybe a string of jet, obsidian, or onyx. You should also try a regular layout using crystals that aid digestion.

Eyes
Traditionally, many crystals are associated with curing eye infection and aiding weak eyesight – this is partly a reflection of just how common serious eye problems were before the advances of modern medicine. Aquamarine, beryl, emerald, and blue chalcedony in particular are recommended to help strengthen weak eyes.

COMMON PSYCHOLOGICAL PROBLEMS

Addiction	Amethyst	Phobias	Chrysocolla, citrine, prehnite, rutilated quartz, sodalite, blue tiger's eye
Anxiety	Pink chalcedony, opal		
Anorexia	Topaz		
Depression	See p. 81	Paranoia	Sugilite
Low self-esteem	Onyx	Rage	Aventurine, peridot
Mood swings	Lepidolite	Shyness	Rhodonite
Obsession	Green jasper, obsidian	Worry	Amazonite, apophyllite, charoite, red jasper, malachite, pink opal, onyx
Psychosomatic illness	Pink chalcedony		

Eczema — Lay antimonite on the affected area and focus on the crystal's healing energy.

Headache — Lie in a darkened room with one of the following crystals over your third eye chakra: amethyst, dioptase, emerald, larimar, magnesite, or smoky obsidian.

Indigestion — Agate, antimonite, aragonite, chrysocolla, citrine, epidote, jasper, and topaz are all said to aid digestion. In general, yellow and orange crystals and those associated with the sacral chakra, often have properties that aid the intestines and stomach.

Menopause — Wear moonstone.

Menstrual cramps — Wear chrysocolla, malachite, moonstone, or serpentine – or lay the crystal on your back.

Self-healing — Wear alexandrite, chrysoberyl, or larimar.

Trauma or shock — Malachite, obsidian, or rhodonite on the heart or solar plexus chakras, or wherever you feel it is appropriate.

Wound healing — To hasten post-operative healing wear amber, garnet, obsidian, or rhodonite next to the skin.

CHAPTER FOUR

At home

One of the subtlest and yet most effective uses of crystals is around the home. If well-placed, their calming vibrations will have all kinds of beneficial effects, encouraging good energy into the home and deflecting negative energy.

Crystals are often beautiful objects in their own right. A large quartz cluster or amethyst geode makes an eye-catching visual statement and its vibrations can subtly transform the atmosphere of your home. Smaller crystals, too, placed in groups for display, or carefully dispersed around the house, will have a noticeable and positive effect on everyone who crosses your threshold.

Well-designed crystal placement has all kinds of beneficial effects – bringing love, luck, and security into your home. But you do need to pay attention every time you add a crystal to your home, taking note to see if its effects are good or bad. Start slowly and build your crystal displays, adding one or two when the mood takes you.

Although many western Feng Shui consultants include crystals in their work, crystal placement in the home or office is an art still somewhat in its infancy. They are said to represent the energy of Earth – an important ingredient of the practice – but usually when crystals are referred to in standard works on Feng Shui, what is meant is cut-glass crystal.

Moving into a new home

The first thing you want to do when you move into a new house is clean it from top to bottom. Cleaning your new home will certainly help to re-charge and energize its atmosphere, but using crystals as part of your cleansing and claiming process will be even more effective. Below are five further steps you could take.

One: Clean
Clean your house. Repaint and re-carpet where necessary. Get rid of anything the previous owners have left behind that you don't want.

Two: Smudge
Using dried American sage, go around the whole house starting at the bottom, filling each room with smoke and scent. Make sure you get into the very top and very bottom corners. And don't neglect the basement and the attic if your house has them.

Three: Make a racket
If you have small children handy, get them to help. Using a drum, a bell, or anything else that comes to hand such as a cooking pot and a wooden spoon. Make a racket throughout your new home, again starting at the bottom. Clapping is good, too.

Four: Clear quartz
Cleanse two single-terminated clear quartz crystals. Put them in the sun for a day and in the light of the full moon for a night. Programme one to rid the house of any negative energy and one to fill it with good energy.

SELLING YOUR HOME
If you are trying to sell your home, it's important to make sure its vibrations are as positive as possible. Have a look at pp. 96–7 for tips on how to harmonize the atmosphere. In addition, you will want to be attracting money, so try keeping malachite by the front door. To hasten the sale, meditate on a fire opal and keep that next to your malachite.

Five: Crystallize it

Wearing or carrying two grounding crystals (see p. 48), take your single- or double-terminated clear quartz from room to room, again starting at the bottom and moving up to the top. As you do so visualize dark energy being sucked out of the house into your quartz and drained down into the centre of the earth through your grounding stones. Visualize each room filling with white light from the crystal. Leave a grounding stone in the centre of any room that feels as if it needs further draining, and return the next day with your quartz points.

WARNING

Crystallizing your home can be a very draining exercise, so make sure that you are well-grounded and feeling strong before you start. When you finish, put away all the crystals you have used and take out a fresh one – either red or black. Sit still with your eyes closed and imagine all of your energy gently reeling back into the centre of your being. Do this by pulling it in with each breath. Afterwards, you should stay indoors, eat a good meal, and go to sleep. Don't put yourself in any energy-depleting situation.

CRYSTAL ROMANCE

A rough red jasper crystal in the corner of your bedroom will help to reinvigorate your love life (see p. 98).

Pinning down your house

Use crystals to stabilize the atmosphere of your home and protect it from bad energy. Placing crystals in the corners of a room or around an entire dwelling has the effect of creating a cage of positive vibrations. This is called gridding.

If you live on a single floor, you can simply put a crystal in each corner of your dwelling – choose crystals such as black tourmaline, smoky quartz, or clear quartz.

Alternatively, pointing four double-terminated clear quartz towards the earth will have a powerfully grounding effect on the whole place. These crystals will drain any negative energy that comes into your home and connect you to the energies of the earth – you may need to tape the crystals to a wall. If you do so, make sure the points are free. If you can, put a fifth crystal in the very centre of your home, also pointing down. This last crystal is not absolutely necessary, but helps to stabilize the grid.

If you live in a high-crime area, try using sardonyx on the ground floor instead. You may also want to place this stone at the windows or any other place that you feel is vulnerable to attack. Obviously, sardonyx is not a substitute for practical crime-prevention measures such as locks.

If you live in a multi-storey dwelling, use the four grounding crystals on the ground floor by all means, but think creatively about what crystals you want to use to grid your upper floor with – if you can, put these crystals near the roof. Single-terminated crystals pointing into your house will bring in good energy.

HIGH-RISE LIVING

These days many of us live with our feet well off the ground. With the growth of populations in cities, the only way to go is up – so we find ourselves living in high-rise apartment blocks. This disconnects us from the energy of the earth, but you can counteract this uprooting by putting grounding crystals – smoky quartz, clear quartz, obsidian, onyx – in the four corners of your apartment. Earth energy is represented by all crystals in general, as well as stones, houseplants, and water. Practitioners of Feng Shui often use a tray of salt crystals to represent earth energy.

GRIDDING CRYSTALS

- *Clear quartz – attracting good energy, deflecting bad*
- *Sardonyx – against crime*
- *Black tourmaline – grounding*
- *Selenite – calming protection*
- *Citrine – energy and abundance*

LEFT *black tourmaline, rough*

Clear quartz is always a good bet, but if you want your home to be especially harmonious try amethyst; or if you feel you lack physical energy, try jasper. As always, monitor the effects of these crystals and change them if you think they are too strong.

You will need to cleanse your gridding crystals every month or so – just after the new moon is a good time for all beginnings.

Sick buildings

Sometimes sick building syndrome is caused by the materials used in the original construction. Sometimes a simple lack of ventilation can be the problem. Both of these causes need to be dealt with directly and do not require the use of crystals. However, when a private home seems to suffer from bad energy, the reasons can be quite hard to pin down and crystals can work an effective cure. There are essentially two kinds of bad energy: overactive or stagnant. Active energy typically runs in lines, but stuck energy can be felt in patches.

GEOPATHIC STRESS

This is disruptive energy caused by features in the environment such as underground water, sewers and tunnels, power lines, mines, and quarries. Railways and motorways can cause great stress also. Maybe the shape of the landscape itself is to blame. For example, if your home faces straight into a high hill or a narrow valley, you may experience negative energy in many ways. Chronic conditions or situations that seem to repeat fruitlessly are also often signs of geopathic stress. Some examples include continuous rowing with loved ones, being accident-prone, or depression. Refer to the panel to the right for further symptoms.

Counter geopathic stress with crystals such as amazonite, amethyst, aventurine, black tourmaline, fluorite, kunsite, larimar, obsidian, smoky herkimer, or smoky quartz. Put the crystal where it will block the stress – and cleanse it frequently.

COMPLAINTS CAUSED OR EXACERBATED BY GEOPATHIC STRESS
- *Insomnia and nightmares*
- *Infertility*
- *Chronic fatigue syndrome*
- *Migraine*
- *Asthma and eczema*
- *Arthritis and rheumatic disorders*
- *Cot death*

ELECTROMAGNETIC RADIATION

We are surrounded by electromagnetic radiation as this is what powers most of the natural world. But those of us who live in urban or suburban areas are exposed to high doses of man-made electromagnetic radiation, which may cause health problems. Power lines, phone masts, streetlamps, electricity sub-stations, and heavy-industry sites may contribute to poor health.

Counter electromagnetic radiation by placing black tourmaline, fluorite, kunzite, lepidolite, smoky quartz, or sodalite between you and the source of radiation.

RADIATION PROTECTION
Counter man-made electro-magnetic radiation by placing readily available crystals such as black tourmaline, smoky quartz, and fluorite between you and the source of radiation.

SHA QI

Modern Feng Shui practitioners would classify both geopathic stress and electromagnetic radiation as Sha Qi or Dragon Lines. Sha Qi is also caused by sharp angles pointing at your home or within your home. This moves in straight lines or in spirals and you can use crystals to bend, deflect, or absorb it, just as you would bend a ray of light. Sha Qi moves quickly. Feng Shui works by slowing down or speeding up energy where necessary.

Counter Sha Qi with:

The classic counter to Dragon Lines is a multi-faceted cut-glass crystal – however using real clear quartz crystal is far more powerful. Hang it facing the Dragon Lines. The crystal will deflect the Sha Qi and exude positive energy. You may need to cleanse the crystals used quite often at first.

BAD AND STAGNANT ENERGY

When energy feels old and cold and stuck in your house, there may be a number of causes. Cemeteries, sites of murders or executions, or some other form of violence may have left disruptive energy traces, or you house may be above a reservoir of underground water. If you believe in such things, you may even have a ghost. Whatever the cause you may experience this as a cold patch.

SIGNS OF BAD ENERGY

Inside

- *Piles of clutter*
- *Cracks in glass, brick, and plasterwork*
- *Recurring mechanical and electrical breakdown*
- *Accident blackspots*
- *Cold patches*
- *Spots where you seem to argue more often*

Outside

- *Ant and wasp nests*
- *Lightning-struck trees*
- *Gaps in hedges or avenues of trees*
- *Infertile fruit trees, cankers, and twisted trees*
- *Bare patches on lawns – moss, silver weed, and fungi*
- *Stunted vegetable patches*

THINGS THAT LOVE SHA QI
If you are trying to locate a line of bad energy in your garden, look for bindweed, ivy, nettles, docks, thistles, foxgloves, ferns, and nightshades, which all like Sha Qi. Cats, owls, snakes, slugs, and snails also like Sha Qi. Cats may even choose to sleep on Sha Qi – in fact, they are very effective at absorbing bad energy.

Dowsing for trouble

Dowsing is most often used to locate underground sources of water. The dowser holds a forked stick and walks slowly over a given area. When he or she passes over the water source, the stick flips. This is all about using your body as a tuning fork that is sensitive to the type of energy given off by water. But you apply the same technique to other kinds of energy.

You may find that you are good at dowsing – people are often surprised at how easy it is. The key is to stay neutral and relaxed. You should be in a meditative state – alert and observant, but not involved.

MAP DOWSING

Dowsing a map or a floor-plan can be a good way of broadly locating troublespots in your home. If you have a topographical map, so much the better. Follow the same procedure as the one for dowsing, but this time simply hold a crystal pendulum over the paper. Dowsing in this way, using a map, will point you in the right direction, but you should still try to dowse the actual physical spot.

LEFT *The pendulum is dark orange carnelian.*

CHOOSING A PENDULUM

Pendulum crystals are available in most crystal shops. Choose one that you feel comfortable with. Try out a few. It should not be too light, and the chain or string should be about 24 cm (10 in) long. Even if you go in thinking you're going to buy a rose quartz you may come out with something quite different. Clear quartz is always a good bet.

Prepare the crystal

You should cleanse the pendulum in exactly the same way you do any other crystal.

Prepare yourself

Holding the pendulum in the palm of your hand, close your eyes and breathe gently through your nose. If you have a formal grounding exercise, do it now. Otherwise, simply imagine that deep roots are growing from your feet right to the centre of the earth. Imagine all the negative energy you are carrying flowing down the roots and out. Then imagine positive earth energy flowing up through your body. This process need only take a minute or two, but you should feel centred and grounded when you are finished. Your mind and body should feel neutral.

Programming your crystal

Pendulums tend to swing clockwise or counter-clockwise, but they can swing in circles or ellipses, and some people simply receive straight lines, both to and from the body and side to side. You need to decide which direction is "yes" and which "no". Hold your pendulum in whichever hand is comfortable away from your body. Hold it over your knee and set it gently swinging. Let it swing in neutral for a while. Now think or even say "yes" and see which way the pendulum moves, then try "no". Keep on experimenting until you feel you know how to 'read' your pendulum.

Dowsing the house

Now go from room to room and test negative and positive responses with the pendulum.

Choosing a crystal

To determine which crystal energy will alleviate the bad energy, identified by your pendulum, in a particular spot, hold the crystal in your spare hand and see if the pendulum becomes less negative or neutral – if neutral, the pendulum will stop swinging. You may need to try several crystals to see which works best for you.

Harmonizing your home

Once you have located any sources of stress and countered them with the appropriate crystal, it is time to encourage some good vibrations into your home. Try a few crystals at a time and see their effect on your household before adding more.

Hanging clear quartz crystals in the window so that they send rainbows of colour into your home is both beautiful and draws in positive energy. To bring in good vibrations try placing a large slice of agate or an amethyst cluster near the front door.

Copper is the metal traditionally associated with the goddess Venus and crystals that contain a trace of it are often remarkably effective at harmonizing vibrations. Try placing copper chalcedony, malachite or, if you are feeling extravagant, azurite malachite in the most used room in the house.

COMBATING DISCORD
If your household seems to be suffering from discord, place rhodonite in a central position. These are crystals of reconciliation that help blocked communications to flow again.

Fuchsite, which is often difficult to locate, is helpful for dysfunctional families, releasing people from un-healthy roles and unknotting co-dependent situations.

SWEET SUGILITE
Said to be the "New Age" crystal, sugilite encourages love and sharing.

The gorgeous violet crystal sugilite (see below left), discovered by Dr Kenichi Sugi in the 1940s, is a lovely thing to have in your main room. It encourages love, attentiveness, and sharing. Emerald is also said to bring domestic bliss and ensure good, long-lasting relationships. Citrine is always good to have around because it has a cheerful vibration, as well as attracting prosperity – place a citrine cluster on your dining room table and watch conversation blossom.

The tourmaline family of crystals is particularly helpful for establishing harmony. Because the vibrations do not clash, you can have a group of different-coloured tourmalines together. Put them somewhere central, such as a coffee table in the living room or on the kitchen table, if that is the most used room in the house. Brown tourmaline is excellent for family commitment and teamwork; watermelon tourmaline helps love and friendship blossom; black tourmaline keeps your feet on the ground, dissolves blockages, and protects from negative energy; red or pink tourmaline encourages chit-chat and a relaxed social atmosphere; green tourmaline keeps you open to new encounters and full of the wonders of life; and blue tourmaline helps easy, truthful communications.

KINSHIP
Grouping families of crystals together can help to keep their vibrations in harmony. Green tourmaline (above top) and black tourmaline (above bottom) encourage open and harmonious communication.

In the bedroom

To get your crystals working for you quietly and efficiently, deploy them in your bedroom. Some people swear by putting single- or double-terminated clear quartz under the mattress as a way of renewing energy while you sleep. Remember though that your bedroom is an especially sensitive area. While you are sleeping you are at your most open to influence, so you need to be very selective about which crystals you bring into your sleeping chamber. As has been mentioned previously, it's a bad idea to have too many different crystal vibrations, because they may conflict and actually cause a chaotic atmosphere, rather than a calming one. This is especially true in your bedroom. Stick to one or two types of crystal and experiment to see how they affect you. Your own reactions may not follow the rulebook, so it's a good idea to take some notes of your sleep and dream patterns over a period of a fortnight or so. You need to give them time to work, and then you need to monitor their ongoing effect.

If you have trouble getting to sleep, put one of these crystals under your pillow – amethyst, chrysoprase, green tourmaline, lapis lazuli, lepidolite, mica, or sodalite. Remember to cleanse and programme it first.

If you have small children who have trouble getting to sleep, try hanging one of the sleeping crystals in a mobile above the bed. If your child is being woken by nightmares, try amethyst, peridot, charoite, or chrysoprase under the pillow. If they are old enough to understand, explain what you are doing and the psychological impact of a protective amulet should help prevent the bad dreams.

Your bedroom should be a sanctuary, shutting out the turbulence of daily life, and allowing you to sleep, dream, or play in a calm and cosy ambience. To create a soothing atmosphere, grid it using amethyst, peridot, or chrysoprase in each of the corners of the bedroom. To pep up your sex life put carnelian, garnet, red jasper, or rhodochrosite under the mattress (or in the corners of your room). For real power, put a ruby under the mattress and watch the fireworks begin.

DREAM EXERCISE

- *Choose one of the following crystals, which are said to enhance dreaming: alexandrite, amethyst, jade, malachite, moonstone, or one of the tourmalines.*
- *Cleanse it, then programme it by holding it in your left hand and saying something like, "Help me find wisdom in my dreams."*
- *Charge it by leaving it in the moonlight for three nights.*

- *Before you fall asleep place the crystal on your third eye and focus gently on its energy – imagine this flowing into your mind and flooding your body with its colour. This doesn't need to take long.*
- *Put the crystal under your pillow or in a glass of water beside your bed.*

ABOVE *amethyst*

Sacred space

As spirituality becomes more personalized and more important to people in the 21st century, creating a special place in your home for meditation, devotion, and worship has never seemed more natural.

In many parts of the world – India, China, and Japan, for example – every home has its altar, a place for quiet contemplation and reconnection with matters of the spirit. Creating a sacred space will have a profound effect on the general atmosphere of your home, bringing harmonious, airy energy into your everyday environment.

Choosing the right crystals for your altar is entirely a matter of intuition. You may want to limit the number, however, to those that are especially important to you – either they have reached you through mysterious synchronicity or they have helped heal you in special ways. Having a single crystal for meditation can help you focus and concentrate your mind enormously.

To create your sacred space, first cleanse the area as you would cleanse your whole home as described on pp. 86–7. Collect together a few objects that have spiritual significance for you – sculptures, pictures, a rock, a feather – anything that you feel connects you to your centre and to the world of spirit, however it is you visualize it.

CRYSTALS FOR MEDITATION

Crystals associated with the crown chakra are the best for connecting to universal spirit.

■ *Amethyst*
■ *Celestite*
■ *Clear quartz*
■ *Diamond*
■ *Jade*

Crystals connected with the third eye chakra are best for finding wisdom.

■ *Amethyst*
■ *Azurite*
■ *Fluorite*
■ *Lapis lazuli*
■ *Sodalite*

RIGHT *(left to right) aquamarine, blue lace agate, turquoise, sodalite, lapis lazuli (two pieces), celestite*

In the garden

Crystals are naturally at home in a garden. They will exchange energies with the earth and with the plants around them in a mutually beneficial arrangment. You can bury them in the soil or use them as part of your display. Hanging crystals from trees can add sparkle and joy to your backyard, and a gorgeous cluster or geode can form a beautiful centrepiece. Remember that amethyst, rose quartz, and turquoise may fade in the sun, so they are not a good choice for garden displays.

A PROTECTIVE SHIELD

To create a protective cage of energy around your whole property, grid your garden as you would your house (see pp. 88–9). Plant five single-terminated clear quartz crystals with the points just peeping through the surface of the soil – one in each corner of the garden and one in the very centre of the space.

You could also grid separate sections of your garden. For example, flower beds and vegetable patches, or eating areas.

EARTH CLEANSING

One way of cleansing crystals is to bury them in soil – you may want to do this with crystals that you feel have accumulated particularly large amounts of negative energy. Leave the crystals in the ground for a month, from new moon to new moon. Take them out and rinse them in fresh water in the usual way.

GARDEN CRYSTALS

- *Prehnite, the South African crystal, is said to be good for the garden, helping to harmonize all the natural energies.*
- *Tourmaline and zeolite are said to boost plant growth and protect crops.*
- *Moss agate is known as the gardener's stone. It helps to attune you to the plant energies.*
- *To enrich the soil, plant boji stones in the garden and allow them to disintegrate.*

RIGHT *moss agate*

CHAPTER FIVE

At work

The effective application of crystals at work can improve your productivity, help develop better relationships with your colleagues, and protect you from stress.

We spend a lot of time at work, and we expend a lot of emotional and mental energy there. We meet lovers, make friends, and discover enemies. It can all be a bit of a soap opera, but maybe that's half the fun.

However, most of us would give quite a lot to feel a little bit more in control of our careers, our workspace, and our own emotional responses. Crystals will never allow you to manipulate other people, but they will help you maintain a tranquil, creative, and productive atmosphere around yourself and your work station. They will also enable you to attract positive energy and avoid negative energy.

If you are a decision-maker at your work, think about deploying some larger crystals, which will help the entire workforce to communicate better and work more effectively together.

Thinking of it in the abstract, money is a form of energy. Crystals can help you to attract this cash energy in the form of career, business opportunities, and liquid assets.

Your work space

Creating your own personal space at work, and maintaining your boundaries, is an important part of modern life. In particular, if you work in an office you can use the subtle energy of crystals to enhance your working environment.

Introduce crystals gradually to your work area, since some may have quite a powerful effect. For example, if you use a computer, take special note to see if it is adversely affected. Although certain crystals are recommended to combat electromagnetic radiation from computers (see p. 91), they may actually interfere with the electronics. So be careful of strapping a huge

PLACING THE STONES
Grounding
Clear quartz or smoky quartz single-terminated crystals, or jet at the corners of your desk near the floor, help ground you and give you energy.

Stones for computers
Computers emit continuous electromagnetic radiation and if you are sensitive, you will find this quite draining after a while. One of the following crystals between you and the screen will absorb some of the radiation, but don't rely completely on your crystal. Make sure you take regular screen breaks.
- *Sodalite*
- *Fluorite*
- *Lepidolite*

Moving energy
To get energy moving in a sluggish office, hang crystal prisms at the window.

LEFT *black tourmaline*

smoky quartz cluster to the top of your machine. The same warning applies to your colleagues. You may introduce a crystal that facilitates communications, such as chrysoprase, and find instead that everyone's talking instead of working.

ORGANIZE YOUR SPACE

A highly effective tool for creating a good office environment is 'gridding'. This means putting crystals at the four corners of your desk or your office – or even the whole building (see pp. 88–9). The smaller the space to be gridded, the smaller the crystals should be. Think proportionately. In general, the best energy for gridding is grounding energy, so try using smoky quartz at first.

Take four single-terminated smoky quartz crystals and cleanse them thoroughly, then programme them to ground your efforts in reality and bring you success (see pp. 52–7). Tape one crystal, pointing upwards, to the inside of each leg of your desk. If you are doing a whole room, tape one crystal to each of the four walls, leaving the tips free.

Concentration and calm
An amethyst geode on your desk will help you to stay calm and focused on your work. It will also help with communication.

Money
Putting malachite in the four corners of your room will draw money into the business.

Decoration
Use big crystals as bookends or paperweights.

Sentinel stones
You can charge two large protective stones – granite, flint, or marble, for example – so that they allow in friends and repel enemies. Place them on either side of the door.

Going into business

Setting up a business takes courage, determination, planning, hard work, intelligence, and luck. If you intend to employ people or you are dealing with customers and clients, you will also need diplomacy and charm.

After the initial excitement, it's easy to become bogged down in paperwork and distracted by minutiae. Keeping ahead of the competition means keeping an eye on long- and medium-term strategy, as well as the day-to-day running of the business.

To do all this it sounds like you need to be superman or superwoman – but in fact quite a lot of people do. The plumber, the childminder, the artist, and the multimillionaire are all running businesses – and they all need similar skill sets.

Undoubtedly, you will have both strengths and weaknesses. You may be a brilliant salesperson, but hopeless at planning ahead. Using the power of crystals, you can bolster your strengths and minimize your weaknesses. Look at the different crystals referenced on pages 110–13 and choose eight or more that you think will help you . The areas in which you are weakest need the biggest boost, so you should try to wear or carry the relevant crystal with you. To

BUSINESS PROGRAMME
After cleansing all of your crystals thoroughly (see pp. 52–5), programme each one separately (see p. 57). Ideally, spread the programming over a week or so, focusing on one crystal a day – don't do them all at once, since each crystal will have a specific purpose.

If you are moving into new premises, cleanse the atmosphere with single-terminated clear quartz crystals before using your special business crystals. Do this by putting a point in each corner of the room and leaving it for a week or ten days.

Keep the crystals that you are not using in a special drawer. It's best to give them all a little space to breathe, so if you can, don't allow them to touch. Unless otherwise suggested, take them out only as and when you need them.

BELOW *(top, left to right) tiger's eye, citrine (second row) raspberry garnet, topaz, chrysoprase (third row) amethyst, labradorite, bloodstone (bottom) lapis lazuli, acquamarine, malachite*

CRYSTALS FOR BUSINESS

Getting started
There are two crystals that every start-up business should have: citrine and tiger's eye. Both these crystals are good for get-up-and-go energy. Citrine brings intelligence and tiger's eye stability. Put them in the wealth corner of your work – that's the far left corner from the door of the room. Keep them charged by putting them in the sun once a month or so.

Innovating/Creating
For inspiration, keep a small amethyst on your desk or in your pocket. If you want everyone to feel inspired and creative, invest in an amethyst geode for the office. Wear an amethyst ring on your left hand if innovation is an important part of your work. For imagination, try aquamarine, labradorite, or fluorite.

AIR OF AUTHORITY
If you need to project good sense, wisdom and maturity, wear lapis lazuli on your right wrist.

For dynamic creativity, try antimonite or citrine. Topaz is one of the stones of the sun, and as such focuses that solar, creative energy. Use it whenever you feel physically tired, lacking inspiration, or if you really need to get things done.

Marketing/Selling

For direct sales, malachite is the best crystal. Wear it on your left hand or around your neck over the throat, whenever you have to go and sell yourself or your wares – it will draw good deals and money to you. Malachite is also good for general business success, so you should always have a piece at your place of work.

Strategic planning

Every business needs a plan. When you are creating your business strategy use lapis lazuli. It is a wisdom crystal, bestowing common sense and good judgement on those who wear it. It will help you keep a steady hand on the tiller also, as it is a crystal of leadership. Keep it on your desk or better still wear it as a piece of jewellery and keep it next to your skin.

Accounts/Money

When it comes to the accounts, use your tiger's eye, a grounding crystal that is great for sorting out details. Tiger's eye is generally a good crystal for business, helping to maintain stability and productivity.

Attracting wealth is one of the oldest uses of crystals – amulets to encourage prosperity have been found in ancient Egyptian tombs. In general, green crystals are associated with money. A basket of green crystals – for example aventurine, chrysoprase, light green jasper,

and nephrite – in the far left corner of your desk or your room will help you prosper. Choose one of these to carry when you need to generate more income – or put one in the till.

Day-to-day details
As well as aiding concentration and organization, agate has long been considered a good luck stone. Fluorite is also said to aid concentration and help you to focus on what's necessary.

CONSOLATION
Keep a bowl of your favourite crystals handy, so that you can hold them when you feel stressed.

Managing people

Good staff are the key to good business. When you're hiring people you need to be able to listen to your intuition and make sound assessments. You'll need to be able to read people, also, and learn how to delegate successfully. Lapis lazuli will give you wisdom and amethyst will heighten your intuition and help you make good judgements.

Delivering the goods

Whether it is crystal pendants, consultancy, or computer programming, you will need to deliver your goods or services on time and on budget. A lot of entrepreneurs are excellent at starting something and not so good at finishing. By the time it comes to actually doing the job, they are bored and thinking of the next thing. Garnet will help you to overcome obstacles and see you through to the finish. Wear it if you can, as it is also a stone of good fortune.

Bloodstone can also be useful in this context. It is an all-round good luck stone, once carried by Roman soldiers to protect them from harm, staunch wounds and to overcome enemies. Wear it for courage, determination, and fortitude.

Risky ventures

Successful risk-taking means successful risk-assessment. So once you have thought out your strategy using your lapis lazuli, you should carry a gambler's lucky amazonite or a green quartz.

Finding your true path

Crystals can be used to help you with all kinds of decision-making. Clearing your mind, focusing your thoughts, and allowing your own subconscious or higher mind to direct you is a process that works using simple visualization. But with the addition of crystals, you will find it easier to focus.

For this exercise, place the crystals directly on your skin under your clothing. Wear comfortable, loose clothing and make sure the room is warm enough as you may find your extremities getting cold.

Use fewer rather than more crystals, since you will need to spend time concentrating on each one. As with most crystal work, the choice of crystal is largely intuitive, so you could substitute amethyst for topaz and smoky quartz or onyx for obsidian.

Here are some ways that you might encounter your crystals during your meditation.

- You see a shining dark pool surrounded by ferns. The pool is as dark as obsidian. What do you see in it or reflecting off it?
- You walk through a shaft of bright light. What do you see?
- Across your path comes a healthy fox with topaz eyes – a friendly fox, who stops to speak to you. What does the fox say?

THE EXERCISE

There are three crystals recommended for this meditation. If you intuitively want to replace any or all of them, then do so.

Topaz is placed on your forehead. Since ancient times this crystal has been associated with the planet Jupiter, the planet of wisdom. It will help you to focus on your own inner abilities and guide you in the right path in life.

Clear quartz is placed on your solar plexus. This crystal helps you see the way ahead clearly and unemotionally. It's energy shines a light on your circumstances that allows you to make balanced and harmonious decision that will benefit you rather than you putting others needs before your own. It is better to place crystals directly on the skin, however, for illustrative purposes, the crystal has been placed on the t-shirt in the picture opposite.

Obsidian is placed on the base chakra or the pubic bone. This crystal reconciles you with your own darker side. By understanding your own nature, you can make better choices and behave with greater integrity.It can also help to dissolve mental blocks.

- Lie on the floor and place your stones, topaz, clear quartz, and obsidian, as indicated (see opposite). Tell yourself that you are going to visualize your way to your true vocation. Ask the question out loud, "What is my true path in life?"
- Close your eyes and focus simply on your breathing for a while. Try to relax your whole body, starting with the feet.
- Once you have complete relaxed, feel the energy from each crystal in turn. Breathe it in with each breath. Allow your aura to fill with the mingled energy of all the crystals (see p. 72).

- Now begin your visualization. In your mind's eye, see yourself walking along a sandy path, through a sunny wood. You see trees and flowers, and hear the sounds of birds singing and a rustling breeze.
- This is just the beginning of your walk, so carry on adding details as you go. Don't strain – your story will unfold. Try to encounter each stone that you are using, starting with obsidian and ending with topaz. Treat it as if it's a real organic experience. You don't have to believe that stones have spirits for this to work because this is an imaginative exercise.

Starting a new job

The first day in a new job is usually pretty over-whelming. All those new names and faces; all that new information – and you're trying to make the right impression at the same time. It's good to start feeling calm, centred, confident, and relaxed.

You will need to be receptive. During your first few days at the new job, you will want to be absorbing information about the people you work with, the politics of the place, and about the job itself, of course. Even if you are thrown straight into some heavy responsibilities, you will want to keep your antennae up to figure out the kind of environment in which you have found yourself. That means keeping at least part of your awareness open for information.

VISUALIZATION FOR KEEPING COOL

Before you go into work, make some time to centre yourself and clear your mind. If you have created a space for contemplation in your home, sit there before breakfast. Take your rose quartz in your right hand and your sodalite in your left (pictured right).

- *Close your eyes and focus on the crystals. Breathe gently, focusing on the breath as it comes in and out of your nose. After a while, you will find that you are clearly feeling energy from the crystals. They should be warm in your hands.*
- *Visualize a pink glow around the quartz. This is a glow of new friendship and warmth. You will want to be sending out friendly vibes to other people. Imagine this glow surrounding you. If you have any sticky encounters during the course of the day, touch the quartz to remind you of this warm feeling.*
- *Next, visualize a pale blue glow around the sodalite. This is the crystal of information gathering. Ask the crystal to help you not to be judgemental, but to be wise; to keep an open mind, but not to be gullible. If during the day you feel you are being misled or misconstrued, touch the sodalite and remember the blue glow.*
- *After you have finished your visualization, eat a good breakfast.*

STONES FOR INFORMATION GATHERING

- *Sodalite – good for processing information and learning what's useful*
- *Aquamarine – for seeing the good side of situations and attracting good responses*
- *Calcite – for analysis and filtering false information*

CRYSTALS FOR BEGINNINGS

Keep one of these on your right side. New businesses should also programme one of these crystals.

- *Citrine*
- *Tiger's eye*

Communications

Meetings, interviews, general chat and phone conversations are the lifeblood of most businesses. People need to be good listeners and good speakers to get on in most jobs. Even if you only have meetings very occasionally, it's a relief when they run smoothly – egos are stroked, good decisions are made, and everybody gets to leave on time.

INTERVIEWS

So often people forget one crucial factor during an interview: you have to listen. You need to pay attention to what the interviewer is actually saying and respond accordingly. Naturally, you should also be feeling your most self-confident and attractive.

For good communications, carry blue chalcedony on your left side or wear it as a piece of jewellery (pictured right). This crystal will help you listen and comprehend; it will give you insight into the people interviewing you. After all, you are also going to be making a decision about them. Chalcedony will help you think clearly. Sodalite is a good alternative.

CRYSTALS FOR COURAGE
AND CONFIDENCE
Red crystals will give you courage and yellow ones will boost your confidence. Try amber, carnelian, citrine, garnet, jasper, ruby, or yellow quartz.

CRYSTALS FOR PHONES
When you are on the telephone, moonstone, calcite, and white fluorite will help you think quickly and respond with empathy. They also heighten your intuition, which can be very useful when you are trying to understand what someone is really saying. Place the crystals in a basket or other receptacle next to your telephone. Although pearls are not strictly speaking crystals, a pair of pearl earrings has a similar effect.

RIGHT *blue chalcedony pendant*

Friends and enemies

Maintaining good relationships with colleagues, clients, and customers is the key to a happy working environment. To maintain a harmonious atmosphere, put a large amethyst geode in the middle of the office. If you need to be more surreptitious with your healing arts, tape one of the stones that promotes harmony under the centre of your desk. Try chalcedony, chrysoprase, or lapis lazuli.

LEFT AND RIGHT

Your left hand is your receptive hand, so it is the one you should use for choosing stones and drawing energy toward you. Hold a stone in your right hand for projective energy – creating a shield or sending energy to other people.

DIFFICULT COLLEAGUES

This is a good healing meditation for dealing with difficult co-workers. Try it when you are at home and you have plenty of time when you will not be disturbed.

- *Make yourself comfortable in a seated position.*
- *In your right hand hold a piece of turquoise and in your left a clear quartz. Allow your hands to rest on your knees.*
- *Close your eyes and breathe gently through your nose. Imagine each inward breath is bringing fresh air into your mind and clearing away all the stress of the day. With each outward breath imagine more and more of your mental clutter floating away.*
- *When your mind feels clear, bright and empty, start to focus on the two crystals. By now they may be quite warm.*

- *The clear quartz is giving you energy. Feel it moving up your arm and into your body. Imagine your body filling with the light of the quartz. The energy is warm and soft and forgiving.*
- *Keep breathing gently and enjoy the light.*
- *Now imagine your colleague floating in a bubble in front of you. You don't have to imagine every hair on her head accurately, so do not strain. Just allow the idea of that person to be there in front of you.*
- *Now allow the light that's in you to expand beyond your physical body and to include your colleague in it. Imagine you are both bathed in its warm energy. Stay like this for as long as you like. If your colleague is a real enemy, this could take some time. Imagine the light is cleansing both of you, washing away your conflict and bringing about peace.*

- Imagine the turquoise in your right hand is beginning to draw in that peace. In your mind's eye, imagine it glowing with this newly found peace – light is filling the turquoise. Let all the positive energy you have just summoned concentrate itself in the crystal.

- When you are ready open your eyes, then drink a glass of water and shake out your arms and legs.
- Take the turquoise to work and either keep it in your right pocket – or if it seems appropriate, give it to the person who has been bothering you.

CHAPTER SIX

On the move

Wearing or carrying crystals is a tradition as old as humankind itself. In many cultures today, the family wealth is still worn as gorgeous, amuletic jewellery by men, women, and children.

Once you begin to work with crystals, you will find that you are attracted to certain types of crystal. You may notice that it is always certain colours that attract you, or a particular family, such as quartz. These are personal crystals and you should pay close attention to your own instincts. They may contain energy that is especially beneficial for you.

There are other, more formal, ways of choosing personal crystals. For example, there is the tradition of birthstones for each month and for each sign of the zodiac. In India, it is common practice for Hindus to wear the appropriate stone for the moon or rising sign. Native Americans may carry totem stones and Aboriginal shamans carry their own clear quartz magic stone (see pp. 30–1).

You may choose simply to carry a crystal in your pocket so that you can caress it, or you may want to wear some crystal jewellery. Whatever you choose, remember that these crystals are meant to protect and strengthen you. Do not wear too many different types at the same time as the vibrations may clash.

Jewellery

Wearing your crystals in the form of jewellery is an expression of identity as well as a powerful healing tool. If you choose the right crystals, this is one of the best ways to feel the real effect of its energy. Crystals worn as jewellery anywhere on the body work protectively.

NECKLACES

A ring of crystals around your neck radiates energy up and down the body – this is very powerful. Modern witches often wear a string of amber when they practise magic. Round or tumbled crystals are considered to be the most gentle, whereas rough crystals can be quite powerful. A necklace of crystals is strong energy, so don't wear it round the clock and be sure to cleanse it regularly.

PENDANTS

You can specifically target your throat, heart, or even the solar plexus chakras with single stone pendants. Wear a lapis or turquoise at your throat for effective communication; rose quartz over your heart to attract and give love; and amber over your solar plexus for power and protection.

RINGS

Wear rings that are open at the back for maximum effect – although you will still get the crystal energy if they are not. At first, wear one ring at a time to see if they have any effect (see also pp. 130–1).

EARRINGS

Crystal earrings work on the upper chakras, helping our mental processes and intuition. Try amethyst for imagination and citrine for clarity of thought.

BELTS

The fashion for jewelled belts comes and goes, but like necklaces they are powerful energy boosters. Native Americans often wear turquoise belts connecting them to the sky and water spirits. A belt will stimulate your sacral chakra and your base chakra, grounding you to the earth in a positive and energizing manner.

ANCIENT WARMTH
One of the oldest semi-precious jewels, amber imparts confidence and warmth to the wearer.

Birthstones

Wearing the correct birthstone concentrates and strengthens your personal energy. Wisemen or wise-women used to prescribe birthstones for their clients right up until the "Scientific Revolution" of the 17th and 18th centuries. In the 19th and 20th centuries birthstones simply turned out to be a good way of selling more jewellery. Since the rediscovery of crystal lore, practitioners have been investigating the potential of healing birthstones.

PLANETS AND SIGNS

According to Western astrological tradition, birth-stones were determined by the ruling planet of your sun sign. Until the Renaissance, astrologers were often also herbalists, healers, and alchemists and they

Sign	Month	Modern Crystal	Traditional Crystal
Aries	Mar 21–Apr 20	Diamond	Diamond
Taurus	Apr 21–May 20	Emerald	Emerald
Gemini	May 21–Jun 20	Alexandrite	Agate
Cancer	Jun 21–Jul 21	Ruby	Ruby, Pearl
Leo	Jul 22–Aug 21	Peridot, Jade	Sardonyx, ruby
Virgo	Aug 22–Sep 21	Sapphire	Zircon
Libra	Sep 22–Oct 22	Opal	Sapphire
Scorpio	Oct 23–Nov 21	Topaz	Citrine
Sagittarius	Nov 22–Dec 20	Turquoise	Lapis Lazuli
Capricorn	Dec 21–Jan 19	Garnet	Garnet
Aquarius	Jan 20–Feb 18	Amethyst	Amethyst
Pisces	Feb 19–Mar 20	Aquamarine	Bloodstone

would use all these skills when prescribing gemstones. Magical treatise from the Renaissance suggest that inscribing the symbol of the planet further strengthened the gem's power. Talismans were created using gem and inscription to ward off evil, attract wealth and love, or gain power. However, astrologers tend to disagree about which crystal belongs to which sign – the following list is a compromise.

In modern times, many other crystals have been assigned to each sign, usually based on colour affinities, which are also part of astrological lore. Some practitioners claim that all crystals are ruled by a particular sign or planet. When choosing your own birthstone, start with the traditional crystal and if that feels wrong, experiment with the modern one.

Colour	Ruling Planet
Red	Mars
Pink, turquoise	Venus
Silver	Mercury
Silver, violet	Moon
Gold, orange	Sun
Navy	Mercury
Blue-green	Venus
Dark red	Pluto (traditionally Mars)
Purple	Jupiter
Black, brown	Saturn
Electric blue	Uranus (traditionally Saturn)
Lavender, sea green	Neptune (traditionally Jupiter)

STONES OF THE YEAR

The 12 months of the year have each been assigned a gem, althought not all experts agree on these. The crystals associated with your month of birth is said to be lucky. Traditionally it should be worn on the index or ring finger; pinkie at a pinch. The middle finger is considered unlucky.

- *January – garnet*
- *February – amethyst*
- *March – bloodstone*
- *April – diamond*
- *May – emerald*
- *June – agate*
- *July – ruby*
- *August – sardonyx*
- *September – sapphire*
- *October – opal*
- *November – topaz*
- *December – turquoise*

Creating your own talisman

Strengthen the energy of your Zodiac or sun sign by wearing or carrying a talisman. Creating a talisman is simple – mainly a matter of timing and willpower. Making a talisman is a form of magic, but it is a also a powerful psychological tool. Touch the talisman whenever you need to tap your own inner core of strength or remind yourself of who you really are. Your sun sign represents your core personality and if you can work with it, you will both feel and be more successful in your day-to-day life.

The best time to make this talisman is on your birthday or at least while the sun is travelling through your sign of the zodiac. You can find this out by looking in the paper. Another good time is when the moon is full or waxing in your sign. You will need to look this up in an ephemeris, which you can find on the internet, in the library, or in a bookshop.

Once you have chosen a good time to make your talisman, gather your materials.

THE METHOD

You will need:
- *The appropriate crystal for your zodiac sign*
- *A piece of silk and a ribbon in the colour of your sign*
- *A scrap of paper preferably also in the right colour*
- *A pen*

When you create your personal talisman, choose a time when you will be alone and not likely to be disturbed. Take your time with the meditation.

The talisman you make should work for one year. Renew it the following year, making sure that you thoroughly cleanse the crystal (see pp. 52–5) and use a new piece of cloth and a new scrap of paper.

- *Cleanse your crystal and leave outside for 24 hours.*
- *The following day, relax and meditate with the crystal in your right hand, turned upwards. Concentrate on its energies. Imagine that the energy of its ruling planet (see chart on pp. 126–7) is focusing on it.*
- *Allow the crystal to become warm in your hand. It should feel almost alive.*

- *When you are ready, draw the symbol of the planet on your scrap of paper.*
- *Wrap the paper and the crystal in the silk and tie it with the ribbon. Now your talisman is ready. Wear it around your neck when you feel you need extra protection, or carry it with you in a pocket or purse.*
- *Do a grounding exercise (see pp. 48–9) or go to sleep for a while.*

Indian Astrology

The Hindu tradition of gem therapy dates back thousands of years. The *Garuda Purana*, which reached its final form between AD 500 and 1000, is one of the earliest know catalogues of crystals and their uses.

RINGS OF POWER
Taureans and Librans may find wearing diamonds empowering. Virgos and Geminis benefit from emeralds. Wear the ring on the corrrect finger for maximum benefit.

Today, Hindu astrologers, who are known as *jyotishi*, prescribe a particular crystal to be worn on a specific finger to strengthen or soften a person's character. This is usually based on the moon or rising sign and ruling planet of the person in question, but you can try it with your sun sign.

Many *jyotishi* advise against wearing either blue sapphire or large perfect diamonds under any circumstances. In fact, it has been claimed that the high levels of divorce in the West are due to our penchant for diamond engagement rings.

CRYSTAL THERAPY

To find the right crystal to wear to reinforce your natural strengths, look up the ruling planet of your birth sign on pp. 126–7 and find the planet below. Wear a ring containing the crystal on the correct digit. Try to make sure the ring is backless, so that you have continuous skin contact with the crystal. If you know your rising sign and moon sign, you may also want two rings containing those crystals.

Planet	Crystal	Alternative Crystal	Digit
Sun	Ruby	Red Garnet	Ring
Moon	Pearl	Moonstone	Ring
Mars	Red coral	Bloodstone	Thumb
Mercury	Emerald	Peridot or green tourmaline	Little
Jupiter	Yellow sapphire	Citrine	Index
Venus	Diamond	White sapphire	Ring
Saturn	Blue sapphire	Lapis lazuli	Middle
Rahu	Hessonite quartz	Agate	Little
Ketu	Tiger's eye	Turquoise	Little

Personal protection

Wearing a crystal that creates a shield of protection around you is one of the most potent ways of using crystal energy. Traditionally this is one of the most important uses of magical crystals. They work by repelling energy away from your aura.

Many crystals have a protective effect and you may well prefer to choose one of your own rather than one from this list. Remember, when you choose this crystal, it should have a kind of outward vitality rather than an energy that turns inward. The best place to wear this crystal is over your solar plexus, which means you will need a longish chain. Alternatively, a crystal necklace of any length is also highly protective.

Once you have chosen your crystal, cleanse it thoroughly. The next step is to charge it with positive energy. The best way to do this is to leave it in full sunlight when the sun is at its highest for about three hours – you may want to do this several days in a row. Do not leave your crystal out overnight, or substitute moonlight for sunlight; it is the full power of the sun that you really want.

Now it's time to programme your charged crystal. Hold it in your left hand and visualize yourself and your crystal surrounded by a bright, white light. Imagine that light expanding until it extends about one meter (3 feet) around you. This is your psychic shield. Now tell yourself and your crystal that whenever you wear it, this shield will automatically snap into position. Repeat this exercise as often as necessary, especially if you feel the power of the crystal weakening.

SOME PROTECTIVE CRYSTALS
- *Agate*
- *Nephrite*
- *Serpentine*
- *Smoky quartz*
- *Turquoise*

THE BLUES
Blue crystals were thought to connect the wearer to the sky and the sea, empowering the individual with spiritual energy.

Long-distance travel

Human beings have always made journeys. We have travelled for business, on pilgrimage, to flee wars, and to follow livestock. Wearing a general protective crystal, such as jet, apache tear, or clear quartz is a good idea when travelling. Yellow crystals, such as amber and cat's eye, are also said to be good for journeys, since yellow is the colour of Mercury, the god of speed. There are also specific crystals which are associated with specific journeys.

If you are travelling in troubled regions, take chalcedony with you. It is said to protect the wearer against injury. Orange zircon is also good for helping to avoid injury.

If you are travelling by water or flying over water, carry a moonstone or aquamarine, the sailors' gems. Wear a beryl for protection against storms and seasickness.

To enhance your enjoyment of travel, try mookaite, the Australian gem that is said to imbue the wearer with the spirit of adventure.

AQUAMARINE
This beautiful gem is a form of beryl and was only classified separately and named aqua (water) marine (sea) during the Renaissance. However, in ancient times it was already thought of as the mariner's amulet, protecting him against the mighty power of the sea.

PROTECTIVE GLOW

Lustrous glistening, known as chatoyancy, is a quality to look for when you are choosing any protective stone, especially those for travel. This movement within the crystal has stimulated many legends, since chatoyancy deflects negative vibrations. It used to be said that a demon or an angel lived inside the chatoyant stone. Cat's eye, star ruby, star sapphire, moonstone, tiger's eye, opal, and sunstone are all examples.

ABOVE *(clockwise from the top) moonstone, tiger's eye, sunstone*

Commuting and pollution

Traffic jams, delayed trains, mobile (cell) phones, air pollution, and plain old rudeness – today's commuter has quite a lot to contend with going to and from work. Carrying your personal crystal or a comforter in a pocket can be a great way to take a little bit of tranquillity with you.

Crystals are never going to stop the effects of environmental pollution, but they can help make you less vulnerable to its ill effects. Since crystals work through their electrical radiation, they are particularly useful against electromagnetic radiation from equipment such as mobile phones. However, take note that a strong crystal may have a weird effect on some electronic equipment. If your mobile phone starts acting up whenever you put your lump of kunzite by the earpiece, try a different crystal.

If you commute regularly, carry one of the protective crystals listed on p. 132 on your right side and a crystal for tranquillity on your left. Don't weight yourself down with too many crystals: you may end up sending out or attracting rather jumbled energy. Two crystals that have been well-cleansed and programmed should be enough to protect you from a regular amount of hassle from fellow travellers and keep you feeling calm. Don't forget to take into account any jewellery you may be wearing.

Many, many crystals are suitable for calmness (see right). This is because of the type of clean, simple energy that crystals give out. You will find that some work better for you than others. Try them out in the shop and take note to see if your energy changes.

STONES FOR TRANQUILLITY
- *Amethyst*
- *Aquamarine*
- *Aventurine*
- *Blue tourmaline*
- *Chalcedony*
- *Chrysocolla*
- *Coral*
- *Daimond*
- *Kunzite*
- *Lepidolite*
- *Malachite*
- *Obsidian*
- *Rhodochrosite*
- *Rhodonite*
- *Sapphire*
- *Sardonyx*
- *Sodalite*

AGAINST ELECTROMAGNETIC RADIATION AND POLLUTION

The most widely used crystals for protection against electromagnetic radiation are fluorite, lepidolite, kunzite, and sodalite.

If general pollution is a problem, try amazonite, aventurine, diamond, smoky quartz, and black tourmaline.

Some crystals work against both. Try aquamarine, aventurine, beryl, and turquoise.

LEFT *(clockwise from the top) sodalite, smoky quartz, black tourmaline, aventurine*

Crystal directory

This is a list of the most widely available crystals plus a few that are simply excellent. Those that are harder to come by have asterisks.

Crystal	Colours	Chakra	Uses
Amazonite	Green to bluish	Heart, throat	Healing, soothing, calming, counters geopathic stress
Amber	Yellow, golden orange	Solar plexus	Protection, creativity, solar energy
Amethyst	Violet	Third eye	Dreams, spiritual work, stress relief, meditation, healing aura, energy
Antimonite*	Grey	Crown, heart	Dynamic creativity
Apophyllite*	White, yellow, pale green	Heart, solar plexus	Powerful healing, absorbing negative energy, rebalancing
Aquamarine	Blue	Throat, third eye, crown	Divination, relaxation, creativity, removes blocked energy, growth
Aventurine	Green, blue	Throat, heart, solar plexus	Prosperity, abundance, fertility, optimism, healing emotional wounds
Beryl	Yellow, golden, blue, red	Crown, solar plexus, sacral	Intellect, decision making, optimism, dynamism
Bloodstone	Green spattered with red	Solar plexus	Confidence, strength, control over your life, luck, cleans aura, energy
Blue lace agate	Blue	Throat	Feminine energy, peace, soothes headaches, relaxation

Crystal	Colours	Chakra	Uses
Carnelian	Red	Base	Intuitive talents, sexual energy, magic
Chrysocolla	Bright blue	Throat, heart, solar plexus	Balances emotions, relieves depression, emotional healing
Chrysoprase	Sea green	Heart, throat	Meditation, calming, gives perspective, detox
Citrine	Yellow, orange	Solar plexus, sacral	Increased physical and mental energy, hope, new beginnings, prosperity
Diamond	Clear	Crown, heart	Connection to spirit, fidelity, truth, insight
Emerald	Green	Heart, throat, third eye, crown	Love, harmony, protects against violence, communication, truthfulness, trust
Fluorite	Violet	Third eye	Creativity and inspiration, mental abilities, strengthens aura, confidence
Garnet	Red, pink, orange	Sacral and base	Passion, courage, fertility, prosperity, joy, vitality, protection
Hematite	Black	Base	Grounding, absorbing negative energy, healing, balances energy flow
Jade	Green, pink	Heart	Long life, prosperity, good fortune, health, longevity
Jasper	Brown, red, sandy, green	Base, sacral	Pursuing goals, ambition, courage
Jet	Black	Base	Protection, divination, grounding
Labradorite	Black with blue	Base, throat	Imagination, releasing inhibitions, self-confidence, self-knowledge

Crystal	Colours	Chakra	Uses
Lapis lazuli	Dark blue	Throat , third eye	Psychic protection, love, peace of mind, wisdom
Lepidolite	Purple, pink	Throat, third eye	Counters electromagnetic pollution, clears mental blocks
Malachite	Dark green	Solar plexus, heart	Good fortune, business success, protection from accidents
Moonstone	Opalescent	Crown, sacral	Lunar energy, psychic matters, clarity of thought
Moss agate	Green	Heart	Gardening, new friends, reveals deceit
Obsidian	Black	Base, third eye	Grounding, inner strength, protection, dissolving pain
Onyx	Black, white, brown, yellow	Solar plexus, sacral, base	"The stone of the ego", stops us from being easily led, inner strength
Opal			
Common	Opalescent	Crown, sacral	Self-esteem, protection
Fire*	Red, orange, yellow	Base, sacral	Success, sexual energy, inner fire, high spirits
Green*	Green	Heart	Healing of all kinds, sleep
Pink*	Pink	Heart	Social skills, warmth, a light touch
Peridot	Green	Heart, solar plexus	Healing, inspiration
Quartz			
Clear	Clear	All	Focusing energy for any purpose
Rose	Pink	Heart	Love, friendship, joy, self-healing

Crystal	Colours	Chakra	Uses
Smoky	Pale grey to brown	Base	Grounding, dissolving pain
Red jasper	Red	Base	Passion, courage, sexual energy, action
Rhodochrosite	Pink	Heart	Love, compassion, positive feelings
Ruby	Red	Sacral, heart, solar plexus	Fire, pure energy, joy, protection
Sardonyx	Black, brown, red	Base	Gridding, protection, personal empowerment, stability
Sodalite	Blue	Throat	Wisdom, communication, organization, protection from radiation
Sugilite*	Purple	Third eye	Wisdom, spiritual love, healing
Tiger's eye	Brown	Solar plexus, base	Grounding, protection, energy balancing, meditation, starting new ventures
Topaz	Clear, blue, brown	Solar plexus, throat	Truth, mental clarity, common sense, justice, spiritual strength, cleansing
Tourmaline Black (schorl)	Black	Base	Grounding, protection against radiation
Blue	Blue	Heart	Self-expression, harmony, truth
Verdelite	Green	Heart	General healing, sense of wonder, joy
Watermelon	Green and pink	Heart	Attracting love and tenderness, friendship, compassion
Turquoise	Green, blue	Crown, throat, third eye	Protection from psychic attacks, reconciliation, divination

Index

Acknowledgements

Gaia Books would like to thank Earthworks and Caroline Roberts who lent us crystals to use in the photographic shoots. They would also like to thank the photographic models – Caron Davis, Caroline Roberts, and Lisa Ruggeri; Roishin Donaghy for hair and makeup; Lynn Bresler for indexing and Kathie Gill for proofreading.

Picture credits

Special photography © Octopus Publishing Group Ltd/Ruth Jenkins; p. 10 Octopus Publishing Group Ltd/Guy Ryecart, p. 17 Corbis/Reuter Raymond; p. 22 Getty Images/Robert Harding World Imagery; p. 25 Mary Evans Picture Library; p. 26 The Picture Desk Ltd/Dagli Orti; p. 28 Bridgeman Art Library/Museum of London, UK; p. 31 Corbis/Werner Forman; p. Photodisc p. 93 Alamy/Ace Stock Limited